THE REAL SPIN
ON TENNIS

THE REAL SPIN ON TENNIS

Grasping the Mind, Body, and Soul of the Game

◆　◆　◆

Jack W. Broudy

ICS Books
Merrillville, IN

Published and distributed in the United States by:
ICS Books, Inc., 1370 E. 86th Place, Merrillville, IN 46410
800-541-7323

Edited by: Jill Kramer
Designed by: Jenny Richards
Cover design: Jeremy D'Arcy and Christy Allison
Interior and cover photos: © 1997 Bobby Bretell

Library of Congress Cataloging-in-Publication Data

Broudy, Jack
      The real spin on tennis : grasping the mind, body, and soul of the
  game / Jack W. Broudy.
        p.   cm.
     ISBN 1-57034-082-X
     1. Tennis—Study and teaching. 2. Tennis—Training. I. Title.
GV991.5.B74   1997
796.342—dc21 .   96-39534
                                                      CIP

ISBN 1-57034-082-X
00 99 98 97   4 3 2 1
First Printing, June 1997

Printed in the United States of America

◆ ◆ ◆

To all of the dedicated, hard-working present, past, and future pros; the "soul pros"— young and old—to whom tennis is not just a job, but a self-expression and a labor of love. You are helping people to enhance their lives.

◆ ◆ ◆

Tennis Bliss...Master the Game

Jeremy D'Arcy

CONTENTS

FOREWORD

As part of the editorial process, I had the opportunity to watch Jack give many, many lessons to girls and boys and men and women of all ages, levels of experiences, and temperaments. The common denominator that was present during each of these lessons was the enthusiasm that was displayed by both coach and student.

Tennis is truly a labor of love for Jack, and his students view the game as a way of life—not just as a recreational sport or mode of entertainment. Jack teaches his students that the "real" game of tennis needs to come from the heart and the soul—and not just the body. I've seen kids who would not necessarily be considered natural athletes evolve into great players because they have grasped the concept of "holistic" tennis so completely.

So many parents have commented to me that their kids have not just enhanced their tennis and improved their competitive skills by taking lessons from Jack, but have grown as human beings, as well. Their maturity, focus, and powers of concentration have increased to such an extent that their grades have improved immensely, they get along better with friends and family members, and they show greater respect for their opponents, themselves, and the game of tennis.

Similarly, adult students make strides that are as dramatic as that of the kids, often progressing from being "C"-level players into "B" and sometimes "A" players in an amazingly short period of time. And, they display the same enthusiasm and youthful outlook that the kids do. Many adults have exclaimed, "I can't believe it! I actually feel like a pro. I never even knew I had that kind of athletic ability before!" Jack's methods really do make people excited about the game!

This book is a comprehensive, all-encompassing compendium of Jack Broudy's life in the tennis world—comprising everything he's learned—both the hard and the easy ways. He's one of the only coaches who's not only paid his dues as a teaching pro, but also on the junior, college, and professional tours. By using this work (which has involved years and years of dedication and perspiration) as your guidebook and your helping hand, you can avoid wasting time, toil, and money on the wrong approach to learning tennis.

You're fortunate to be reading *The Real Spin on Tennis*. It will give you all of the tools you need to become a "real" player—and to grow as a person, too.

— *J. Kramer*
  Editor

ACKNOWLEDGMENTS

I'd like to thank, first and foremost, Jill Kramer, my sweetheart and soulmate, without whom I might never have finished this book. She was my editor and my inspiration, giving me the confidence, support, and love to finish what I had started. Thanks from the bottom of my heart...for reminding me that I had something to say.

◆　◆　◆

I'd like to give special thanks to my family: David (dad); Dory (mom); and my sisters, Frances and Nadya; who all gave me support throughout my junior, college, and pro careers. Both of my parents made many sacrifices, financially and timewise, for my growth and education as a tennis player and a human being. (I'd also like to pay homage to *all* the parents of young tennis students who try to educate their children appropriately.) My dad always said that it was important for me to learn the game of tennis because it would be a source of enjoyment and healthy entertainment throughout my entire life. Right you are. Thanks, Dad.

I'd like to acknowledge and thank all of my students throughout my 20 years of tennis coaching and instruction. They were, and still are, my good friends and my reason for coaching. We've all grown in mind, body, and spirit together. We always believed in one another, which gave me the courage to continue in my profession. It would be impossible to mention one student without mentioning them all, but the message goes to each and every one of you.

Thanks to all of my close friends and colleagues for their confidence, support, and loyalty: Jon Mayberry for his help and trust, for always being there for me...and for being a great model for the interior photos; John Newman for his friendship and for his editorial help; Dr. Michael Forman and family for letting me use their beautiful court and for their complete confidence in my abilities; the Rileys; the Platts; the Wilburns; the Troglers; the Mahans; the Lings; the Clarks; the Lees; the

Hongs; the Hemingways; the Chengs; the Moallemis; the Levys; the Kouries; the Niemans; the McDowells; the Susnows, the Yus; the Fitches; Dr. Margot Aiken; George Moungvong; Eliot Schencker; Dominick Corigliano for being my yoga mentor over the years; and Jeremy D'Arcy, Jenny Richards, and Christy Allison for their design talents, which they applied so well to this book.

I'd like to pay homage to the Pacific Ocean and my beloved surfboards for keeping me energetic, lucid, and high-spirited throughout the long, hot teaching/writing days.

I'd like to thank my partners and opponents for all those years of growth, challenge, and excitement. It all made my life much more enriching and fulfilling. Finally, I'd like to pay my respects to all of my teachers and coaches who helped me find my way.

Thanks to all of you!

Author's Note:

All of the instruction in this book is written for right-handed players. Lefties, please reverse the instructions.

Please check the glossary in the back of the book for the definitions of any unfamiliar terms.

Chapter One

FIRST THINGS FIRST

"...Good...Good...Lift it up...Good...There...Good...Big follow-through...Higher!..C'mon, get lower...Bend!...No...Yeah... Good... Okay...Footwork...C'mon, get movin' you lazy...Way to go... Racket back...Earlier!...Forget that one...Keep it in the court... Okay...Good...All right...Good job! Let's stop on that one."

A hearty high-five, and you're on your way home—$40 poorer, and absolutely no smarter or better!

◆　◆　◆

Have you ever gone home from a tennis lesson that sounds like the one above and asked yourself, "What did I learn today?"

Have you ever wondered, "Is that it? Just a few tips on form, hit a lot of balls, and now I'll be a good tennis player?" or "How many balls and how many years will it take me to improve?"

If any of these thoughts have ever crossed your mind, take a look at the list on the next page. It may sound familiar to you.

◆　◆　◆

The 10 Classic Cliches of Tennis Instruction

1. Get your racket back. Earlier!"
2. Follow through."
3. "C'mon, low to high. Hit more topspin."
4. "Bend your knees!"
5. "Snap your wrist." [On overheads and serves]
6. "Don't take your racket so far back."
   [On return of serve]
7. "Toss higher." [On serve]
8. "Punch your volleys—out in front!"
9. "Watch the ball."
10. "Step in. Transfer your weight."

The list above represents what I call "shotgun" or "cliche" instruction. A coach shouts out a series of commands, so one of them is bound to work, right? Probably not. And that's why I had to write this book. There is so much more to the game of tennis, and there's a better way to explain it to people who want to improve—people like *you!*

Believe me, tennis *does* make sense if you're taught how to play the right way!

There's no question that there are exceptional pros out there—those who are trying to make a difference. They are exploring and expanding the game of tennis. They are the true teachers and students of the game, and I salute them. On the other hand, there are a lot of people doing financially well through the sport who are no more than promoters and businesspeople—or ex-tournament players. In fact, I recently read that one of the best-known tennis coaches in America charges $1,500 an hour—and he's never even played "A"-level tennis! How could someone like that really know what it's like to be down triple match point in the second round of the NCAA tournament, with all the emotional turmoil that that entails? How could he do justice to a student who wants to know what that experience is like?

On the other hand, there are many players who graduate from college, having played tennis since they were five years old, and then decide, "Okay, I'm going to coach." Unfortunately, they don't know anything about *teaching;* they started playing tennis so young that it's become second nature to them—and they just can't relate to what it's like to be a beginner. Now, how could someone like that know how to teach a student about choking? He or she has probably never choked! Remember, it's *your* money that's being poured down the drain on teaching methods such as those above—so really think about what you're paying for.

The Real Spin on Tennis is about breaking away from antiquated and/or impractical teaching techniques and breaking through to the smartest and most logical way to play your best—by understanding the game as a pro does (in some cases, better). "Grasping the mind, body, and soul of the game" indicates that you have to take full responsibility for integrating all aspects of yourself to become a real player—or a real coach.

This book is targeted to anyone who wants to understand the game fully. Coaches, parents of juniors, tennis enthusiasts of all ages, and nationally ranked players alike can learn to put the following information to good use. Basically, if you still have "bad days" on the court, this book is for you. Let me tell you why I think so.

Tennis Is So Easy...

Overall, the way tennis is still being taught really infuriates me. People who should love the game get frustrated at best, and at worst, quit. Many take lessons, practice, and play matches, generally seeing little if any improvement once they've hit their first plateau. In most cases, only the very young players—the ones I call "junior pros"—ever have a chance of looking and feeling like accomplished players. Why? Because they spend all their time practicing. Eventually some of these kids catch on, but only a small portion of them ever realize their full potential. The sad thing about all this is that the game is so easy and could be enjoyed by everyone if they only knew some simple principles and a few tricks of the trade.

These days, tennis is taught through a perfunctory list of instructions. Even the trade magazines reiterate the same old fundamentals. Some coaches vocalize these orders with more enthusiasm than others, but the game as a whole still suffers from a host of hackneyed cliches that we all heard 30 years ago when rackets were smaller, shorter, and made of wood.

It seems to me that for the most part, instructors tend to pick out a few favorite idioms and use them on a continual basis whether or not they apply. For example, I was watching a lesson recently where the student hit a forehand into the net, and the coach yelled out, "Follow through!" Of course the student doesn't question it. He's heard it before. But what does it mean? Where exactly is "through," anyway? Is "through" the same for every ball? For every player? Why did the ball go into the net, and how can the student make sure it won't happen again?

When I walk past a court and I hear this stuff, I just want to run out there, grab the racket out of the instructor's hands, and scream, "Stop! This is not helping. Explain the game!" The ball's going into the net, and there *is* a reason. It's not just a matter of "bending the knees" or "following through." The pro needs to say to the student, "The majority of your balls are going into the net, and here's why...."

Another type of instruction that makes me laugh (and then cry) is when the coach tells the student, a "B" woman, for example, to hit "higher" or "lower" or "Hit more topspin!" C'mon, if the student knew how to do these things, don't you think she would? This reminds me of the time my friend Ben, who was teaching me how to windsurf, yelled (as I sailed farther out to sea), "Sail this way" (back to shore). I yelled back in frustration, "I'd love to. Why don't you tell me how?"

You also might be familiar with the "drill instructors," who move you from side to side yelling, "Good" or "C'mon." Balls are flying everywhere, and you're sweating up a storm, but nothing whatsoever is happening with your game. After you bust your butt for an hour, they tell you what a good job you've done. What good job? *They're* the ones who're supposed to be working! You're supposed to be *learning* something—not making a buddy! Recently, I was watching a teenage girl—an aspiring tournament player—take a lesson, and she was hitting cross-court forehands, side-stepping back to the center of the baseline. She looked pretty good. I came back ten minutes later, *and she was doing the same exact drill,* but she had actually gotten worse! You know, doctors get sued for malpractice all the time. Who's protecting *you?*

Then, of course, there are the "advanced lessons" that purportedly help you with the "mental side" of the game. I'm not talking about reputable sports psychologists such as Dr. Jim Loehr. He certainly has some very sound ideas on the "head game," the mental and emotional aspects of competitive tennis. The advice I'm talking about is the type that comes from many teaching pros, who spout platitudes such as "Concentrate," "Relax," and "Focus."

Sure, those words make sense (in a sense), but they're not *enough.* I mean, if players could "relax" and "concentrate," they would, don't you think? That's why they're taking lessons—to learn. It's the job of teaching pros to provide instruction on the *entire* game, including the psychological intricacies. Everyone gets nervous, granted. But there are clear-cut techniques to overcome and/or deal with those nerves (which I'll go into later in the book). Remember: The best matches that the pros play are those where there's the most on the line, and the biggest shots are made under the greatest pressure. There *is* a reason why some people rise to the occasion, and anyone can learn to do it—especially *you!*

Whaddaya Know?

Ask yourself the next time you drive home from a lesson, "What do I really know now that I didn't know an hour ago?" If you can't take something new home with you and write it down or explain it to someone else, what did you learn? All you had was a glorified workout.

Why do you think you play so well in a lesson, but when it's time to play a match, nothing seems to work in quite the same way? In most cases, it's because in your lesson you're being fed balls at a steady pace, and after an hour your timing naturally gets better—your *timing—not your game!* You still can't hit the "no-pace" ball, the high backhand, or the consistent deep second serve. You have no better understanding of the game, and you haven't necessarily improved your tennis—you've just got your timing down. That doesn't last, as I'm sure you know. There's drilling/practice, and there's instruction/education. Most aspiring players with limited time need more education than they're getting. Knowing the game will increase the value of your practice time two-and threefold.

The most amazing thing of all to me is that students have become so inundated with the type of instruction I've detailed above that **they come to a lesson expecting to hear the admonitions that they already know.** In fact, once they hear them, they decide that this pro must really know his or her stuff, because that's what the other pro said. I can't tell you how many first lessons I've given to people who say right off the bat, "I'm having trouble with my serve" [or whatever]. "I know what it is I'm doing wrong; I need to get my racket back. I need to...."

I say to myself (or to them), "Excuse me, am I supposed to agree with you? What are you telling me? I mean, if you know what you need, what are you paying *me* for? Go hit against a ball machine!" The fact is, if you had the answers, you wouldn't be taking a lesson, or for that matter, you wouldn't be reading this book. You've played the "cliche fundamentals" until now, with pretty much the same results.

So, for those of you who really love the game and are ready for a change, my program is for you! You are sure to find new and better techniques in these pages that will markedly improve your game. Get prepared to finally "understand" the game of tennis. Learn what makes things happen on the court and how you can control them. Learn how to "fix" your topspin forehand before it's too late. Find out how to make all your second serves in a tie-break. See how you can become your own tennis doctor!

Read on, and get ready to look and feel like a pro. This book is an education, a master's, if you will. If you're stuck at a certain level, I will certainly give you the tools to move ahead. You'll be able to grow and develop into an "all-court player," someone who knows what you're doing in all aspects of the game. Since you've even bothered to pick up this book and start reading it, you've already taken the first step to becoming a better player. Enjoy reaching your full potential, on and off the court. You'll find that tennis will enhance your life more than you could have ever thought possible!

But first, let me tell you a little about myself...

How I Came to Understand "The New Tennis"

About five years ago, I crushed the right thumb of my playing hand in a hydraulic lift accident, severing all of the nerves and tendons. I had to stop playing conventional tennis for six months, but I was on the court coaching the day after the accident with the help of my ball machine and my assistant pro and friend, Marc. Little did I know that this "break" would be the turning point for my own game and for my teaching.

A few days after the pain subsided a little and I was off the pain killers, I decided to play tennis with my left hand. I had missed hitting the ball, and I knew it would be a growing experience, at least for my teaching. I was curious to see how I did in a sport I had played well for two decades. Little did I know that it would change the way I feel about the dynamics of the game forever.

I started out against the ball machine—horribly, I might add. I had no control on either side, and I mishit over half the time. Frankly, I was surprised that I was this bad. My racket was "back," I "watched the ball," and I "followed through" nice and high like I was supposed to, and I stunk! I couldn't even run with the racket in my left hand. I could finally relate to some of my beginner, or less naturally talented students, when they would tell me that they were "trying" to do what I'd tell them. So, that's when I decided to experiment with some ideas that I had never seen put into practice or heard of before (and at that point in my life, I thought I'd heard it all). I began to think of the times when I was playing my best. "What did it *feel* like?" I asked myself. I had to start simple and keep it simple, because my left arm couldn't handle much more. I had virtually no coordination.

I started at the service line, where I could get the ball over the net with my left hand by just "bumping" it against my strings. I decided that the most important thing was to first make good contact—a solid hit. I took a very small backswing, leaving my left elbow close to my left hip, keeping my racket face perpendicular to the court, flat to the ball. From there I slowly brought my racket face directly toward the ball. I just "bumped" the first couple of balls. Once I felt comfortable making good contact with the ball in the middle of the strings, I slowly came to a perfect finish and froze in that position. **"Touch and finish"** is what I kept saying to myself. Amazing as it may sound, within half an hour, I was comfortable hitting forehands and backhands from the service line with my left hand!

Starting with "touch and finish," and continuing with additional techniques that are highlighted in the following chapters, I not only became a proficient player with my left hand, but I even *looked* like a pro. Imagine that—I could hit topspin off both sides, a one-handed backhand, a backhand chip, volleys, overheads, and even flat and slice serves—all with my left hand! Keep in mind that my left arm had been completely dormant for 30 years, developing absolutely no coordination or strength (my left forearm was one-and-a-half inches smaller than my right), and within a month I felt comfortable, had pretty strokes, and had fun playing left-handed, with a cast still on my right hand.

It's those principles that I've used to teach myself "lefty" tennis that I have recorded in the pages of this book. The funny thing about all this was that I was always well known in whatever section of the country I was teaching in as an exceptional tennis pro with many ranked players in my fold. I thought that I knew the game as well as anyone. And I probably did. But I was merely a better analyst and communicator than the average teaching pro. I hadn't created a better mousetrap; I had simply become proficient at expressing the same old fundamentals in an interesting way. Those same principles that I had used on hundreds of students—including ranked juniors, college stars, and playing pros, did nothing to help my own left-handed game.

That's when I realized that the entire game, and the way it was taught, had to be scrutinized and revamped if it was to ever become a truly popular sport. I knew that if I could become a competent left-handed player, the average weekend hack could learn to play a good game, and not just get the ball back over the net, hoping that the other guy would miss.

The following chapters teach the "new fundamentals" based on actual lessons and success stories at the pro and non-pro levels. The lessons are incorporated into chapters that will serve as your tennis program, helping you improve at the quickest rate possible. Following the steps will enable you to play better—every time you step on the court. Not only that, you will find that you enjoy your tennis at a much higher level than you ever have before. Tennis will become more of a "full" experience. You'll feel exhilarated and rejuvenated, much the way one does after a rigorous ski session or aerobics class.

This program encompasses the entire sport, from the mind games—the mental and psychological aspects—to the technicalities of strokes. This program will help you learn how to become an integrated "all-court" player, controlling your emotions as well as the ball. And if you've been in a tennis "rut," these lessons will serve to pull you out of it. Just as important, you'll learn to perform at your very best under pressure.

This new information is about today's tennis, which is much different than when I was playing junior tournaments with a Wilson Jack Kramer wood racket strung with gut, costing about $40. Then, rackets had virtually half the sweet spot and less than half the power. Tennis was all about style: "Straight back or the big loop," two-handed or one-handed backhands, and so forth. It emphasized consistency, placement, and finesse. The tennis elite were artists: Bjorn Borg, Jimmy Connors, Chris Evert, Ilie Nastase, Manuel Orantes, and Guillermo Vilas, all of whom, by today's standards, would be considered backcourt players.

Today's game is about efficiency and power. Lighter and longer rackets can generate most of the velocity if used correctly. Today's new equipment makes it possible for *anyone* to play the game—and play it well. However, players are still battling the same problems with inconsistency, physical ailments, and an overall lack of control, strength, and confidence, especially when they play under pressure. Tennis enthusiasts, more than ever, find that they get to a certain level and then reach an impasse. So, if, in your own game, you find that noticeable improvement is slow or nonexistent, it's not necessarily your fault. The fundamentals of the game have changed, and you just haven't been informed. I'm here to tell you that you're about to "break through" to the next level.

I have been fortunate in my life to have coached many players, some from the first time they picked up a racket, through the college and professional ranks. I coached 10-year-old "junior pros" to men's 55-and-over champions. Through my coaching and my own personal experiences with junior, college, and professional tournament tennis, I've discovered what works best for all levels of players, especially through the new perception that I attained as a lefty.

I was always an innovative tennis instructor, just as I was a player, but not until I injured my playing hand did I truly understand the fundamentals of today's game. I found it frustrating and extremely difficult to learn to play with the old principles that I was using to teach myself to play left-handed. I could finally relate to my students who had a difficult time learning the strokes. I knew what I was supposed to do, but my body wouldn't do it.

That's when I began to discover a new set of principles that are logical, easy to perform, and different from the conventional (old) ones. Believe me, if I can learn how to play and feel comfortable and confident with my left hand, which had been completely weak and uncoordinated up until then, then certainly anyone can learn to play correctly with their playing hand.

The only players that I ever see improving through the old methods are those exceptionally proficient athletes who would play well regardless of what anyone told them. They can actually learn by watching. The old teaching style relies on the player developing timing, which takes years to acquire, and can be lost at a moment's notice, usually when the player is under match pressure. Actually, it was one of my students who pointed this out to me. She told me that even though she had only played tennis for four months, she was improving every time she stepped on the court. Her friends who had been playing for years, on the other hand, were standing still because, as she put it, "They never make any significant changes in their game and just seem to be waiting for 'time' to make them better players."

I hate to wait. Don't you?

What You Can Expect

The techniques outlined in this book will enable you to:

◆ Get relaxed and focused for a match
◆ Warm up quickly
◆ Simplify and improve all your strokes
◆ "Fix" your game at any time
◆ Anticipate and move better on the court
◆ Play your best under pressure and win the big points
◆ Improve your overall consistency on the court
◆ Serve bigger, with more spin and better placement
◆ Keep relaxed and focused during a match
◆ Build on your game, allowing you to jump to higher levels

Once you've completed this course, you will fully understand the game and be in complete control of your own destiny as a player. It will no longer be a mystery every time you play a match: "How am I going to play today? Is this going to be an enjoyable afternoon, or am I going to wish I never showed up to the court?" You'll know that you're going to have a positive and growing experience out there, and no matter what situation arises, you're going to deal with it in a way that will make you feel good about yourself. You will be able to really use tennis to enhance your life.

So for those of you who are ready to leave the worn-out world of "racket back early," "low to high," "follow through," "get mentally tough," and don't forget my favorite, "bend your knees," welcome to the new fundamentals of today's tennis. You'll play because you want to—not because you have to (in order to maintain your timing). This is your advanced degree in tennis, which will provide you with a lifetime of athletic prowess, personal power, and pure enjoyment.

Okay. Begin play.

Chapter Two

TUNE UP BEFORE YOU PLAY

How do you get ready for work or school? Do you throw some clothes on as soon as you get out of bed and rush right out the door? Would you feel comfortable or confident if you went about your day without brushing your teeth, showering, or shaving? It's not likely. Many of you probably have a routine that you follow religiously—one that (whether you realize it or not) actually sets the tone for the rest of the morning, afternoon, and evening. If you feel inspired and enthusiastic during your early-morning activities, that feeling will most likely continue; if you feel lethargic and pessimistic, however, things might not go so well. Proper preparation is key—which only makes sense. After all, most professional athletes, artists of all kinds, and even top-notch businesspeople have rituals that they perform on a daily basis to get them in tune for the upcoming day.

Similarly, if *you*—a tennis player—want to get the most out of your practice session, lesson, or match, then prepare like the pros, and get in the habit of doing so every time you step on the court. Rarely do I see that any of the tennis programs, lessons, or clinics mandate a pre-court warm-up, and that's a disservice to you! Pre-game routines vary to some degree from player to player, but the basics need to address the three areas that make up a real player: one's physical body, mental focus, and emotional stability. (I'll go into more detail later in the chapter.)

True "all-court players" learn something every time they play, whether it's during a lesson, a practice session, or a match. And let me tell you: Learning is a skill that can *definitely* be developed. The first thing you must do is create an atmosphere that is *conducive* to learning, one that is separate from the competitive aspects of tennis. You can't learn if you're always competing with yourself and others. It's vital when you're being taught new information that it gets properly assimilated in your mental body, and not just your emotional one. The difference is that the mental body equates to learning, while the emotional body just satisfies the ego.

A match, practice session, or lesson must be preceded by exercises that help your body get warm and limber, and which put your "self" into a "walking sleep"—that is—you become so centered within yourself that you are oblivious to any and all outside distractions or pressures. That's how it feels when a "player" plays the game, and that's why when a pro is playing well, a fellow pro commentating a match will say, "He's unconscious." This walking sleep is crucial to your learning process because it's the condition that brings you closest to "playing in the zone"—playing with your mind, body, and emotions in total harmony. Before you step on the court, first engage in a rigorous, inspired, and active warm-up. This step will physically prepare your muscles, and just as important, will put your mind in the relaxed and focused state that you need to be in when you step on the court.

Before You Hit a Ball...

1. *Shake your bones and get loose (2–3 minutes)*: Go for a short jog, walk, hit a few balls (easily) against a wall or with a practice partner, or even take a hot shower to get your muscles warm and ready for action. Make sure to wear sweats or a warm-up suit when it's cold. When jogging, it's best to first run forward and then side-step and "back-pedal." Once you feel a loose high-step, lift your knees toward your chest and "butt-kick," bringing your heels up behind you. But keep it light, and don't exert yourself. You're building up,

so you want to open your lungs and warm up a bit before you start your stretch. If you're about to compete, this is a good way to work some of those pre-match "butterflies" out of your system.

2. *Stretch and breathe; clear your mind (5–10 minutes)*: Take at least five minutes to stretch. You're about to engage in some rigorous physical activity and passionate play for the next hour or more. Your body needs to be ready to move and react in several different ways and directions. Not only will stretching help you avoid injuries, but it will also get you to move and react more quickly and with more endurance. Another positive by-product of stretching is that it makes you more centered. The best way to get into this proper state of mind and body is to concentrate on your breathing as you stretch, pull your breath in deep and low from the belly to the chest, and exhale fully as you direct your attention to the flow of the exhalation.

   Don't stop at the top of your inhale or at the bottom of your exhale, though. Keep it continuous. Long and strong. Optimally, you want to breathe through your nose—loud. Remember that a big breath equals a big stretch.

   (There's a comprehensive stretching program described at the end of this chapter that is based on Ashtanga yoga, which is a very rigorous and aerobic form of stretching. I have found that this program is best suited for tennis because it stretches you out but doesn't make you lazy or lethargic, as slower forms of stretching and yoga can.)

3. *Establish your focus and composure: visualize (3–5 minutes)*: Before you play, it's important to calm down and let go. This is essential, especially for those of you who are coming from work, school, or any other possibly stressful situation. The more you've rushed to get to the courts, the more you need quiet time to get focused and go within. Meditation can serve as a very useful tool before a match. Surround yourself with white light and positive energy, and silently repeat positive affirmations such as:

◆ "I believe in myself."
◆ "I'm a winner."
◆ "I appreciate and love who I am."
◆ "My game is constantly improving."
◆ "I play my best today."
◆ "I relax, concentrate, and simply let go."

Remember to always put your affirmations in the present tense. If you affirm: "I *will* be a great player" or "I *will* play my best today," then your goal will always be out there in the future, beyond your grasp. However, by voicing your statements in the present, the universe responds to your current positive energy and draws more of it to you. (And you thought this was just a book about tennis!)

You can also *visualize* yourself playing great tennis: serving aces, volleying winners, moving and hitting with good form and fluidity—and having fun. Visualization is a tool that serves as a valuable and veritable "dress rehearsal"—it gives you the "feeling" that you're playing well even before you step on the court. When you become proficient at visualization, you'll "recall" your positive feelings and bring them with you onto the court. This process will start you off with additional confidence, and I'm sure I don't have to tell you how important confidence is to playing well. Well, maybe I do: CONFIDENCE IS SUPREMELY IMPORTANT TO YOUR GAME! Okay, okay, no more yelling—we're trying to *relax* here.

Let me tell you a little more about relaxation, and how it affects all of the elements of your game.

The Benefits of Relaxation:

◆ Enhanced physical performance
◆ Improved reactions and responsiveness
◆ Increased sense of well-being
◆ More enjoyment on the court

Here's an example that illustrates how pivotal relaxation is to your performance on the court:

◆　◆　◆

John, a successful attorney, had a weekly, late-afternoon lesson with me. I had no idea when he showed up for his lesson on this particular day that he'd had to deal with employee problems, equipment failures, and a host of other troubling predicaments. He'd hopped into his car after work, driven straight to the courts, changed into his tennis clothes, and in no time at all was hitting balls with me.

I didn't know at that point what had transpired before the lesson, but I saw the effects after just a few minutes of play. John was frazzled and unfocused. He was overhitting and was overanxious, as if he'd been playing poorly for an hour or two and was now completely awkward and dejected. He moved in a stiff-legged fashion, hard and slow. He was angry and upset with himself, barking out self-critical remarks starting from his *first* missed ball, and continuing to do so on every mistake thereafter.

The standard response to such poor play (and probably what John was anticipating), would have been to offer a lot of technical advice, such as "racket back earlier," or "stay sideways on your (one-handed) backhand," and so on. At best, this would bring about small corrections, but there would be no real turnaround as far as John's basic problem was concerned.

I fed John balls for a few minutes, saw how he was hitting, then waved him into the net. I asked how his day had gone and quickly got the picture that it had not gone well. His problem was, he could not let go of his stressful day at work, so I walked him through a quick solution. We both did some stretching exercises, and I asked him to only think about his breathing as he pulled his breath slowly into his diaphragm and exhaled fully. I told him to keep it rhythmic and continuous, never stopping at the top of his inhale or the bottom of his exhale. We "ran the lines"—that is, we energetically ran along the lines of the court, to and from the net a number of times. Then when we got to the water fountain, I said, "John, soak your head." He looked at me like I

a

was crazy. "That's right," I repeated. "Let the water run over the top of your head and onto your neck. Then close your eyes, and let the cold water run down your forehead and over your entire face. The more direct the better." He did it.

We then headed out onto the court, and what a difference that little "meditation" made! John moved quicker and lighter, stroked the ball with more confidence and fluidity, and really started to enjoy himself. He had previously been too "uptight." However, once he relaxed and freshened up a bit, he was able to really play.

◆　◆　◆

Most people come on to the court thinking about things other than tennis. So, they play poorly and have no fun because they're not relaxed and not completely there. The emotional baggage of the day walks right on to the court with them and limits their play and pleasure. For example, your mind can be full of "static"—thoughts about work, school, or your personal life—and you will not play well or have fun until that static is tuned out. It is a scientific fact that performance is directly affected by attitude. Your mind likes to ruminate and endlessly review things—usually problems. And since you can only process one thought at a time, until you let the rest of the day go you're not really playing tennis—you're simply going through the motions. The fact is, when the body is bogged down by stress, it can't react and perform to its full potential. Physical performance, well-being, and fun all turn on relaxation and focus. Remember, relaxation allows you to make technical changes and, therefore, play better tennis. So learn to relax, and you'll become unstuck.

4. *Get fired up, and get your motor running (1–2 minutes)*: Now that your body is loose and warm and your mind is quiet, you need to get your motor going. You have a vigorous hour or two ahead of you. The stretching and breathing serve to relax you. Now you need to pump your mind and body up so you're not too relaxed to go for it. I've stretched and visualized to the point where I was too calm to compete. I've found, for myself and my students, that if you do

some rigorous cardiovascular work between the time you stretch and the time you play, you'll be relaxed and invigorated at the same time. And that's the best way to play.

Run the lines of the court, jump rope, or jog around the court with vigor. Your physical body needs a "jump start"! Do some sprints, side-stepping and back-pedaling. In short, preview all the moves you're going to use in the game. Just remember, you don't want the first time you run to be during a point. Get ready for action now! Get moving! You're relaxed, so now you can get active and energetic and be ready and able to concentrate. So, get into position, and perform your best.

◆   ◆   ◆

Of course, letting go and being relaxed are easier said than done. Like anything else, relaxation is a learned skill that improves with practice and reinforcement. In time, it becomes a habit, so that when you play, you play calm and loose.

As I mentioned earlier, the proper preparation can, and very often will, determine what kind of day you're going to have out on the court. For example, if John had gotten to the court ten minutes early to stretch and relax, he could have gotten off to a much better and more enjoyable start.

The following stretching program will relax you and let you concentrate on your game. It will allow you to play with enthusiasm and confidence. The keys to playing your game well are simple, and are in your own hands. You want to start playing more consistently and with more confidence and enjoyment, so get in the habit of "warming up" off the court—just like a pro would!

◆   ◆   ◆

J.W.B.'s STRETCHING PROGRAM

STANDING POSES

The Sun Salutation: This stretch is the very best exercise in terms of loosening up and energizing the entire body in the shortest amount of time. Repeat it at least three times before you play. (This salutation to the sun is also a wonderful exercise to do before bed and also when you first wake up as part of your overall fitness maintenance program.)

Stand up straight, chest lifted, shoulders rolled back, exhale.

Look up, arms lifted, inhale.

Head toward knees, exhale (bend knees if necessary).

Inhale, look up, lift top backs of legs.

Exhale to a push-up; elbows in, butt low, no bow in lower back. Chest can be on the ground.

Inhale, chest open, shoulders rolled back, legs alive. Top of toes on ground.

Five breaths, inhale-exhale, fingers spread, shoulders away from ears. Bend knees if you need to!

Inhale, jump or step forward; look up.

Head toward knees, exhale (bend knees if necessary).

Look up, arms lifted, inhale.

Stand up straight, chest lifted, shoulders rolled back, exhale.

LUNGES

This stretch is good for opening the shoulders, the groin, the insides of the legs and hips; and even the lower back.

Legs strong, extended from center; steady breathing.

The Triangle Pose is good for stretching many areas as well: stomach, ribs, shoulders, back, and hamstrings.

Lift kneecaps, strong triangular base; open chest.

Forward Bend/ Arms Over: Shoulders, hamstrings, hips, abductors

1. Stance: Spread legs three to four feet apart. Wide stance. Heels out, toes in (slightly). Clasp your hands together behind your back (pressing your palms together).

2. Roll back shoulders, hands lifted off your butt, inhale. Lift and open your chest.

3. Bend from your waist forward. Bring the crown of your head down toward the ground, and lift your clasped hands over head, and down and away from your back.

4. Slowly straighten up to a standing position, breathing.

Full breathing; move your body out slowly as you breathe—not fast!

SITTING POSES

Spinal Twist: Right knee up, right heel by the right buttocks. Keep your right foot flat on the ground. Left elbow outside right knee. Look up and back. Twist. Try not to let the right knee buckle to the inside. Big-time breathing.

Inhale, lift chest; exhale, twist slowly. Extend opposite leg, toes straight up.

Shoulder Opener: Right arm to inside of right knee, lean forward. Bend elbow around the right leg, reaching back behind knee. If you can, grab the right hand with the left hand (reaching around your back). Now lean forward over a straight left leg, toe pointed up..

Inhale, reach inside knee; exhale and rotate, bend elbow. Grasp hands behind back.

The Frog Pose: This one is good for the lower back, hips, and groin area. Soles of feet together, pull your heels close to your groin. Hold feet with hands, and bring legs down. The end points are your knees. However, don't force them toward the ground. The stretch begins from your upper thighs and groin, and then works out to your knees. Next, lean forward (to where it's comfortable for you), chest first. Try not to round your back. Hold it to a slow count of five. Breathe.

Extend from groin out through knees, slow breathing, no bouncing!

Forward Bend: Straight legs out in front of you. Sit up erect. Knees, ankles, close together. Lean forward and reach for your toes, bending from the waist. Lift up from the waist and then go forward. Spill your chest out over your thighs. Try not to round your back. Hold it and breathe into it for a count of five. This stretch is excellent for the pelvis, lower back, and backs of the legs.

Backs of knees toward ground, knees and ankles close together, lift chest. Tilt pelvis; spread top backs of legs.

Dominick, my yoga master, always says that when stretching, remember these basics:

- Breathe throughout; long, strong, and full inhales and exhales.
- No bouncing!
- Let your breath guide your movement.
- Don't force movement; surrender to it with your breath.
- Feel the stretch.
- Spread from within, to your extremities.
- Keep your eyes from wandering. Focus on the stretch.
- This isn't competitive.

Get in "The Zone," ASAP!

You're not done quite yet. Now that you're ready to step on the court, it's time to take your focus and physical coordination to a higher level. Engage in a five- to ten-minute ritual before you start your warm-up rally, and you'll see dramatic improvement in your concentration powers immediately.

Tennis teachers throw words such as *concentration* and *focus* around as if these are incidental concepts that come naturally to everyone. The fact is, most people never get fully focused. Others can't "get into it" until somewhere in the middle of the second set. Still others can start out focused when they're fresh, but as a match wears on, somehow their attention span and momentum slip away, along with the match.

The "zone," a term used for the deepest level of relaxed concentration, is attained by very few players aside from touring pros. However, this mental state is the essence of masterful play. It is the psychological and emotional state that allows you to play at your highest level of performance. No matter how good you are, or think you are, if you can't get into (or close to) this "zone," you can't play your best. First, you need to get there, then you've got to *stay* there.

"The Zone"

> *"It's really quiet...I don't hear anything. The crowd's a blur, the umpire's a blur, my opponent's a blur....The only thing that's in focus is that little yellow, fuzzy ball. It's the only thing I see. It's the only thing I hear. I love playing tennis."*
>
> — Andre Agassi talking about being in "the zone" on "60 Minutes" in 1995.

I would say that Agassi's recollection of his time in the zone is probably the most accurate, on-the-mark description that I've ever heard. The zone is that "next step" that competitors move to in their evolution as "real players."

Let me give you an example of something that happened to me when I was in the zone.

The story I told you earlier, about how I broke my right thumb and had to play "lefty" for six months, had an even more profound ending. After not playing tennis with my right hand for half a year, I finally started back, gingerly, to play "righty." I rallied once and found that it was still too painful to hit topspin on my backhand, so I was forced to hit slice so there'd be less pressure on my thumb. Also, my serve wasn't quite as big as it had been before the accident. However, my groundstrokes were surprisingly good, almost as if I hadn't taken a day off. In fact, it seemed as if I was seeing the ball better, making better contact with it. I felt that I was swinging with less effort, yet hitting the ball with more authority.

The day after I had rallied for the first time, the tennis director at our club said that we were having a large tennis function, and he wanted me to play in an exhibition the next weekend. I was slightly intimidated, because my thumb didn't feel strong enough to play a match, and to boot, I was going to be playing against someone who I knew was clearly better than I was, even when I was at the top of my game. I played a couple more times that week before the match, but although I felt stronger and quicker, I could still only hit a slice backhand.

The day of the exhibition came, and I did my stretching and visualizing about an hour before the match. Then I rallied with my assistant, playing right-handed and left-handed just for fun. Match time came, and I rallied against my opponent, Paul. I felt okay, but I could tell that he was taking me lightly, so I thought that if I could capture an early lead, I could escape being humiliated in front of my students and the club members.

Well, I played in the zone from the first point to the last. I didn't do anything that was above my ability, nor did I get lucky. What I did was play the best I was capable of on that day. My first-serve percentage was high, and I didn't double-fault. I returned every serve, except for the aces. The only points Paul won were the ones that he hit as outright winners. I played really well and was fully focused during each point. I didn't "over-try," and I didn't lose my focus on the ball. I saw the passing shots and hit them. The ball seemed like it was magnetized to my racket. It was the first time I had ever taken a set off Paul!

That exhibition set was the first time that I realized that my six months of lefty tennis were what would make the difference in my (and my students') focus and level of match play from that day on.

Over the next several months, I consulted with doctors and psychologists on the mysteries of the left and right hemispheres of the brain, which I had read a little bit about in college. The right side of the brain is what's activated when you use the left side of your body, and vice versa. The right brain is the creative, more cerebral one, while the left side activates more practical and mathematic thinking. The left side is "closed," while the right is more "open," which may be why the left-handed players such as Connors and McEnroe hit more of an open-stanced forehand.

In any case, I've been teaching left-handed tennis to my students ever since, and I've seen many of them become grateful denizens of that truly wonderful and mysterious place we call..."the zone."

The Pro-Active Warm-Up

Once you've made it to the court, there are a couple of things you can do before you rally to improve your game, whether it's a lesson, practice session, or match. The following ten-minute program will help you focus even more intently on the ball, while improving your overall game. Along with your pre-court warm-up, it will help put you in that "walking sleep" or "zone," while it increases your coordination and athleticism. Make the time to practice the following exercises before you play, and you'll notice an enormous difference in your concentration and performance.

Habitualize the On-Court Warm-Up

1. *Play lefty for five minutes*. With your racket in your opposite hand (that is, hold it in your left hand if you're a righty, and in your right hand if you're a lefty), start at the *service line,* with your pro or a hitting partner at the opposing service line. Try to keep a rally going from service line to service line. Do every-

thing as if you were playing with your correct hand. Don't just tap the ball over. Start by touching the ball and then coming to a complete finish, gently "placing" the ball in front of your partner's service line, so that he or she can hit it back.

Divide the stroke into two parts. Focus on the "touch" or "bump," then come to your "finish." If you're a two-handed backhander, use two hands. If you're a one-hander, use one. Mirror your full-court game the best you can. After a few sessions of this, you'll find that you can hit topspin and slice, as well. But start with a flat hit the first day or two.

What this exercise does is open, or activate, the opposite side of your brain—the side you don't use, or use very rarely. Also, it helps you focus on the contact point of the ball and your strings. You can't take this nondominant side for granted, and therefore you concentrate more deeply than you normally would. By trying to play perfectly, you remind your dominant side of what it needs to do. Generally, you'll find that whatever flaws you have are exaggerated by your nondominant side. So basically, in this exercise, one side of the body helps teach the other side to play. You must try to use a perfect stroke if you want to get the most out of this exercise. Once you get the hang of it, you might want to start moving back slowly until you're rallying baseline to baseline.

If for some reason you can't play lefty, at least swing the racket around, forehand and backhand. It's better than nothing. And remember, every time you do so, it has a cumulative effect on your game.

2. *Hit righty—short court.* After a few minutes of hitting with your opposite hand, you can go back to your dominant one, but start, once again, with both you and your partner up at the service lines. You need to be able to hit and feel comfortable from every part of the court, not just behind the baseline. Hit easy, with perfect strokes, practicing "touch and finish." No overhitting! Make the balls land between your partner and the net.

Have patience. Don't just block the ball. Stroke it slowly and cleanly. Play as if you were giving a lesson, trying to show someone the most perfect strokes. Use full and exaggerated finishes. If you can hit topspin and slice as well as flat, practice all of these strokes.

3. *Play at three-quarter court.* Finally, before you get to the baseline, play a few balls from midway between the service line and the baseline, trying to hit the ball just beyond the service line. Hit easy, keeping the ball in play. Get comfortable at three-quarter court until you get to a proficient level—this is where many, if not most balls are missed. There is still no need to hit hard. You're trying to control the depth of your shots as well as the direction. Feel the court. Continue to touch and finish.

4. *Full court—at three-quarter speed.* Once you've hit from the midway point for a couple of minutes, you can move back to the baseline and hit full court. Stay in control. Don't hit all-out yet. Get a feel by hitting 60 to 75 percent of your full speed. Generally, players who hit too hard during the warm-up have trouble in the match, if the pace isn't a fast one. Practice your control. You can feel the ball on your strings, and you can feel your stroke better if you swing at a comfortable three-quarter pace. It's also easier to correct any glitches at that speed. Hitting your hardest too early disguises mistakes.

5. *Review: feel the court.* Now you have a perspective from several different points on the court, not just the baseline. This exercise helps you to "feel" the (dimensions of the) court, while it gets you fully focused on both the ball and your strokes. By hitting softly at the service line and three-quarter court, you can feel your stroke easier than hitting hard right away. In this way, you can make minor corrections and smooth

your strokes out early in the day. This type of warm-up is imperative if you want to start playing well on a consistent basis. It will also increase your ability to learn, and therefore speed up the rate at which you absorb new information. The proper warm-up translates into deep focus and improved play and enjoyment—and it takes all of 15 to 20 minutes. Your game, attitude, and day deserve it!

◆ ◆ ◆

We'll continue talking about focus and the zone throughout the book, as it is the basis for performance under pressure. There are additional ways to get and stay in the zone, but this is a great place to begin, even before we start to improve your game. Once you're in this learning mode, you'll grasp the upcoming information much more easily.

◆ ◆ ◆ ◆ ◆

Chapter Three

TODAY'S SOLID AND EFFICIENT "GROUNDIES"

Everyone works on their strokes. It's as if they're obsessed with them: "Am I following though? Do I need a bigger (or smaller) loop on my forehand? Should I be using a more Western grip (that is, a grip that is naturally closed, where the racket face is slanted toward the ground)? Am I stepping across on my volleys? Am I turning enough on my backhand? Do I have enough wrist snap on my serve? Is this the right grip?"

Relax, people, this is not nuclear physics! You're hitting a sphere with a plane. How difficult can it be? Not difficult at all. Every student I've ever taught has had beautiful strokes within weeks of their first lesson, whether or not he or she was a natural athlete to begin with. Mastering the strokes of the game is truly the easy part of tennis. It takes a lot more talent and effort to move, anticipate, and focus, believe me. So, let's keep it real simple here.

What you need to remember is that all styles of stroking the ball have three things in common:

1. The starting point
2. The middle (the point of contact or impact—where things really happen)
3. The finish

Please don't let the terms *backswing* or *follow-through* enter your mind. There's a much better way to view the groundstrokes (the "groundies")—a way that works for everyone, which is going to revolutionize the way you learn how to master them. Basically, you're going to learn the strokes "inside-out," and I mean that literally. We're always going to start from the middle, and then work the stroke out from there.

What benefits can you expect to reap from this technique?

◆ Good strokes, which are easy to reproduce
◆ Consistency
◆ A simple, clear understanding of power, spin, and accuracy
◆ Enhanced rhythm and timing
◆ How to avoid unnecessary movements (hitches), and conserve energy
◆ Reduced tension and injury
◆ Simplicity

Not long ago I gave a first lesson to Brenda, a high-school senior who played on her varsity tennis team and was considered to be a good player. She told me that she hoped to get a tennis scholarship to a top college.

Brenda told me that she had been "pro-hopping" for the past year or so, and was now thoroughly confused about how to improve her forehand. She asked me a series of questions about grips, "loops," open (or closed) stances, and follow-throughs. "So many different pros have told me different ways to hit it," she complained, obviously very frustrated.

I suggested, "Let's hit a few balls and then decide what to do."

We hit for about ten minutes. She moved well on the court, and looked as though she had a pretty good game. Her two-handed backhand was definitely the stronger of her groundstrokes, but her forehand was not as smooth or strong. We met at the net and talked again.

I told her that her backswing (on the forehand) was too big, especially since she was a tall girl with rather long arms. Therefore, her hitting arm started and stayed too far away from her body, making the racket head difficult to control. I told her that she didn't seem to see the "impact point" on her forehand as well as on her backhand. "And finally," I told her, "I think your follow-through varies too much from shot to shot, all depending on where the ball is in relationship to your racket and body. Sometimes you finish looking over your arm, sometimes under, sometimes with a straight arm, sometimes bent, and so on.

"Let's simplify your forehand and see if that helps stop the confusion. First, put this tennis ball under your right armpit. [Brenda is a 'righty.'] "Now, when you prepare for the forehand, just turn to your right. Keep your arm close to your body, keeping the ball under your armpit." She hit a few forehands from the service line that way.

"Next, I'd like you to finish the stroke, with your right shoulder pressed up against your chin. To do this, you'll have to keep your head down and lift your right arm up. Once you finish, the ball (under your armpit) should fall forward onto the court." She swung, and the ball did just that.

"That's it?" she asked.

"That's it!" I replied.

Brenda had the basics down as far as preparation, balance, and timing were concerned. She just needed to keep it simple regarding start, contact, and finish. Once she took the ball out from under her arm, she understood the principles of the forehand: small backswing, long middle, and a consistent high finish, "chin to shoulder" (keeping her head down on the point of contact).

Before we start learning how to master the groundies, I'd like to offer you two suggestions with respect to your practice sessions:

1. Practice in the same way that you would play a match. Don't over- or underhit. Play with a purpose.

2. Take a pad of paper and a pencil to your workouts and lessons. It's good to jot things down that you discover in your practice sessions, as well as in your matches.

Okay, now, let's begin.

Grip Check

First we'll talk a little about grips and their relationship to the strokes. It's really not that important what grip you use, so long as it works for you and you understand the pluses and minuses of each one. There are five main grips that are used in tennis today, and they are as follows: the *Eastern forehand,* the *Western forehand,* the *semi-Western forehand,* the *continental,* and the *Eastern* or *full backhand* grips. The grips are designed to contact the ball, giving it natural topspin, slice, or no spin (flat).

This is the Eastern Forehand, the "handshake" grip. The palm is pointed in the same direction as the racket face.

This is the Eastern Backhand, with the knuckles on top of the racket grip. You should be able to press your thumb up the side of the grip ("Don Budge Backhand").

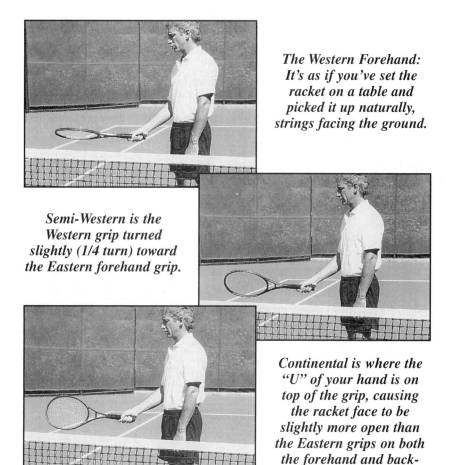

The Western Forehand: It's as if you've set the racket on a table and picked it up naturally, strings facing the ground.

Semi-Western is the Western grip turned slightly (1/4 turn) toward the Eastern forehand grip.

Continental is where the "U" of your hand is on top of the grip, causing the racket face to be slightly more open than the Eastern grips on both the forehand and backhand grips.

The Eastern Forehand Grip

The Eastern grip on the forehand meets the ball naturally as a flat contact, with the racket face perpendicular to the court and flat against the ball. It's known as the "handshake grip" because that's how it feels. This was the "classic" forehand grip when I was growing up, when flat was the order of the day, à la Chris Evert, Stan Smith, Arthur Ashe, and John Newcombe. The advantages to this grip are: low balls are easier to hit, and it's a natural power grip because it hits flat against the ball.

The disadvantages of the Eastern grip are: Sometimes high bouncing balls are difficult to hit in the court, and some players find that it's harder to derive big topspin with the flat face. Also, I would advise strongly against using this grip for the forehand volley; it's too flat. This grip is only for the forehand groundstroke. Although Jimmy Connors uses it for both his forehand and his two-handed backhand, he is the exception.

The Eastern Backhand Grip

The Eastern or "full" backhand grip was, and still is, the best grip for flat and topspin backhands. As you see in the picture, the knuckles of the hand are on the top of the racket grip. Like the Eastern forehand grip, this one makes the racket face flat to the ball, perpendicular to the court, naturally. It is good for one- and two-handed backhands. Many players who want big spin on their serves and are strong enough to derive the sufficient power, use this grip with great success.

The only slight disadvantage to this grip is that slice backhands and backhand drop shots can be a little more difficult to hit than with the continental grip. Stay away from this grip at the net, because like the Eastern forehand, it is too flat.

The Western Grip

This grip (used on the forehand) creates the most closed racket face, which will naturally hit the biggest topspin. The person who made this grip famous was Bjorn Borg back in the early '70s, and his topspin was truly uncanny. Today, several world-class players such as Chang, Agassi, and Bruguera, to name a few, use the Western forehand grip. Other than its usage for big topspin, the Western grip is ideal for high forehands.

The disadvantages of the Western forehand grip are that it is extremely difficult to hit very low balls, such as skidding backhand chips, and it is virtually impossible to hit the drop shot, which requires you to open the racket face during the hit. You'll also find that it is not natural to use this grip to hit flat or chip. Agassi uses this grip for his swinging forehand volleys at net. It is risky (but fun). It's not a grip you bring to net if you want to win.

The Semi-Western Grip

This is the grip that many players today gravitate to for the forehand, because it can naturally create good topspin, hit flat, and can even get under the low balls (at least better than the full Western). It is probably the most versatile grip for today's game. Like the Western, it is very good for high balls because the face stays somewhat closed.

The only disadvantage I can see is that unless you have this racket face mastered, drop shots could still be a problem with this grip. Unless a player has extremely good timing and is very fast, I'll usually steer them away from the Western to the semi-Western grip. Only if you're hitting a swinging forehand volley should this grip ever be used at net.

The Continental Grip

The continental grip is the one held with your hand midway between the Eastern forehand and the full or Eastern backhand grips, opening the face just slightly (more than Eastern grips) for both the forehand and backhand. It is the best and most versatile grip for serves, volleys, and overheads. It is also a perfect grip for hitting the drop shot on either side. Many two-handed backhanders like to use this grip because it is an easier grip to switch to from their forehand, and if they have to, they can chip the backhand as well as hit topspin.

Some players use this for both groundstrokes, although it is very difficult to put topspin on either the forehand or the one-handed backhand. High forehands and backhands can also feel very unnatural to hit with this grip. However, low balls are much easier to get under.

The Contact Point for
Flat and Topspin Groundies

Tennis has always been taught emphasizing stroke production: "Ready position," check your "grip," get your "racket back early" (straight or loop), step forward and "transfer your weight," and swing "low to high," with a "complete follow-through." And, incidentally, "watch the ball." Well, if these things worked, there would be more club players who looked like players, at least when they rally. The fact is, most club players have some kind of elbow brace on their arm and make the game appear very difficult (as opposed to the pros who make it look simple). Surprise! It *is* simple!

It's not that these buzz words and cliches don't apply to the strokes—it's just that none of them describe the *essence* of the strokes. They don't make the strokes happen—at least not by prioritizing them. What I hear pros telling their students is, "Just do these things, and after a lot of practice, you'll be a good player. It takes a lot of practice—years!" The key words here are "a lot."

Well, it seems to me that it takes too much practice for most people to ever get "good." The type of instruction I've talked about above generally only works for the very young and very gifted athletes, the "junior pros." Frankly, many of these kids would probably be just as good without half those lessons. Andre Agassi once said, and I believe it, that Nick Bollettieri was "incidental" to his becoming a player. Many players learn just as well by *watching* good tennis. When I was growing up, I'd watch Stan Smith, Jimmy Connors, and Bjorn Borg on TV, and then I'd practice for three or four hours a day, all summer. By the end of August, I got pretty good. But then I'd lose most of it during the school year. All I really got was form and timing.

Most aspiring players have to practice constantly, or their tennis dramatically suffers. The same applies to pressure situations. I've seen so many player at the clubs and in junior tournaments completely fall apart during matches, to the point where they look totally different from the way they play during practice sessions. Many players can fall down an entire level (that is, from "B" to "C") in just one afternoon.

An understanding of the dynamics of stroke production will mini-mize any fluctuation in your game. You'll always play respectably. It only takes me or my students a few minutes to get back to our game, even after a lay-off. Very often I play matches with only a stretch and a warm-up run to precede them. That's all you need, because you're not just playing with timing. So, get to know the strokes.

Begin at the Middle

All of the strokes should initially be learned from the middle; then you work your way out to the rest of the swing. Everything revolves around the contact point—where, when, and how the strings contact the ball. No matter what style you have, or what grip or stance you hit with, the impact point determines where and how well the ball will be hit. Connors doesn't have one stroke in the game that looks like Sampras's or McEnroe's or Graf's. The results are similar, though, because each one of them does basically the same thing in the middle.

◆　　◆　　◆

So, first discover the middle—the "spot" where contact happens. The following exercise is an absolutely essential one for learning the correct way to hit both forehands and backhands.

(Please note that all of the instruction in this book is being taught from the standpoint of right-handed players. Lefties, you just need to reverse the instructions.)

Stand with your left foot almost flush against the net. Now, with your left hand, place a tennis ball against the top of the net. Next, press your racket up against the ball so the ball is wedged between the net and the center of your racket strings. Notice how your racket looks: paral-lel to the net, top edge pointed almost straight up—that is, "on edge." Look at it!

Press the ball against the net, "on edge." Get a good look at the contact point. This is where you want to be on every hit.

Next, roll the ball over the net by simply lifting the edge up and keeping the racket pushing forward. That's all there is to it! It's the key to life for a backcourt player! Once you can master that contact point, and do it consistently, you'll have the groundstrokes down. Now practice it on the backhand. That "spot" you see from the time you contact the ball to the time you roll it over the net, is the most important three inches in tennis. That spot (those few inches) is always your main focus when mastering the groundstrokes.

Roll the ball over, pressing forward, lifting the edge up.

The Lethal Forehand

Start by extending your left hand across your body, palm facing down. This will help get you turned sideways to the net. It's very hard to know just how far to "turn" on the groundstrokes, and it's an especially hard concept to think about when you're playing under pressure or on the run. Watch the great players; they extend their opposite hitting hand across their body before they hit. Chris Evert probably reached across with the most exaggerated style, but it was beautiful and effective.

Your pro will undoubtedly tell you to turn your shoulders before the hit, but extending that left hand will make it happen naturally. This technique basically helps get your racket back, so there is no reason to take your arm too far away from your side. The farther away your right hand gets from your side, the farther away your elbow gets, and the farther away from the middle your racket face gets—making it more difficult to control. So, keep your elbow comfortably close to your side and slightly bent. Make sure your arm is close enough to your side to hold a tennis ball under your armpit. Remember, it's the turn of your body that creates the backswing.

Your arm is comfortably close to your side, elbow in. Your left hand is extended, which automatically makes your right shoulders turn. Notice the small backswing—the racket is "on edge," that is, the racket face is either perpendicular to the court or parallel to the net.

How (or how far) you take your racket back is not nearly as important as getting under the ball, though. Don't take the racket back too far or too high or straighten out your right arm behind you. That makes it nearly impossible to get under the ball comfortably. Some players take the racket straight back and low. Others "loop" it back, lifting their racket head slightly higher, then circling down (for a flat hit) or below the level of the ball (for topspin).

How far you take your racket back is relative only to getting to the "spot" with the racket face and the ball (and the imaginary net). Something in between works best for many players. If you feel you can make it in time, and you need the power, then go ahead—take it back to whatever degree suits you! I think you'll find that if you start relatively close to the middle, you'll see that you don't need quite as much power; plus, you'll find that your momentum gives you sufficient power to come to a complete finish with good contact.

◆　◆　◆

Another exercise: Try putting a tennis ball under your right armpit, stand at the service line, and hit forehands. Just turn forward into the hit. Start with your left hand extended across your body, and then pivot your back foot, while seeing the "spot." You'll see that you can actually hit the ball accurately and with some pace. Don't overdo the dreaded backswing. It should find itself naturally.

Crucial to your stroke is that the racket head then drops underneath the ball, either by dropping the handle for flat shots, or by dropping the head of your racket below your right sock (for topspin). Remember, as you drop either the handle or the head, keep the racket face perpendicular to the court or just slightly beveled. If you open the face as you get under the ball, you'll hit a lob (I'll talk more about this later).

Drop the racket head below the ball. Your arm is still close to your side; your left hand is extended. Notice the small backswing; the racket is "on edge," as in the case of the forehand.

Go back up to the net again. Now start with the (top) side edge of your racket about an inch below the ball. Then lift that edge up toward the ball until you have the ball wedged between your racket strings and the top of the net. Make sure the strings "press up" against the ball while the edge is perpendicular and on its way up. Generally, contact is best and simplest when it's out in front of your body.

Continue to lift the racket's top edge, rolling the ball over the net. Now, your bottom edge is an inch above the ball. Remember to always keep the face parallel.

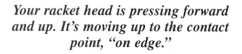

Your racket head is pressing forward and up. It's moving up to the contact point, "on edge."

The finish is variable, seeing that the ball has already left your strings. Generally speaking, it's best to finish with the head of your racket high, above your own head, while you're looking over your hitting arm. Bring the shoulder (of your hitting arm) up so it touches your chin. Try not to ever look under your arm! That is only for extreme topspin, in difficult situations. Touching your chin to your shoulder will help you keep your eyes down and fixed on the ball.

Finish: Eyes down (where the ball was contacted), chin to shoulder, racket "on edge" and high (racket head higher than your own head). Roll the back toe completely, squaring shoulders and hips to the net.

If it helps you to stay loose and hit with more topspin, try finishing with your elbow bent, with the racket edge touching your left shoulder.

Finish variation: Let the elbow bend. Notice how the racket edge touches the left shoulder without rolling over. Stay "on edge"!

Make sure to pivot your back foot completely, to shift your body weight into the hit and stay on-balance. Forget "weight transfer," which is the term that club pros use to tell you to shift your weight forward during the stroke. That doesn't mean anything. Just roll your back toe over. That will transfer your weight sufficiently.

Finally, use the "touch and finish" method to help you understand the stroke. Try to divide the stroke into two parts, in slow motion, so you can stop action (in your mind) at the hit, and then finish. This is also a great method for staying focused on the ball.

Quick Forehand Fix-Its!

— If you're hitting many of your forehands into the net, it's probably because: You're not getting your racket head under the ball.

To fix it: Get under the ball! Relax your elbow. Drop your racket head below your right sock and swing up to the hit. Getting under doesn't mean opening your face. Make sure to keep the racket face "on edge."

— *If you're hitting your forehands long, it's probably because:* Your racket face is too open. You're most likely hitting the ball on your way down with your face open, bottom edge leading, causing the ball to spray up (like a chip shot in golf).

To fix it: Make sure you drop the head of your racket behind you (below your sock—not on the way to the hit), and then come to the hit while your racket is on the way up.

— *Another reason why your forehands might be going long could be:* You're opening your body before the hit (by rotating your shoulders early), causing the racket face to open.

To fix it: Keep your left side down by extending your left hand across your body a little longer. Stay on the ball. Finish "chin to shoulder," keeping your eyes and shoulders facing the contact point.

— *If you're hitting your forehands wide, it's probably because:* You're hitting the inside of the ball, causing it to spray wide (away from the court), inside-out. You're hitting late, or your racket head is dropping, bringing your handle up first.

To fix it: Swing earlier, or try getting the tip of your racket around the outside of the ball. Don't let that ball get away from you! Get *around* the ball.

Tip for intermediate players: Always refresh your memory as to what position the strings and the ball must be in at contact. Roll the ball over the net.

Tip for advanced players: Have someone (or a ball machine) hit you balls over the baseline while you're standing on that baseline. Hit swinging forehand topspin volleys. Take a clean swing at the ball, getting under, coming up to the "spot," and finishing with your racket edge up to your left shoulder. But in your mind, see the stroke in slow motion and "stop the action" at the "spot." Admittedly, this practice takes some inspired focus. However, I've found that most students, after the proper warm-up, can do this with some consistency. It's a simple exercise. You can even vary the amount of topspin on the ball. If you want to take a drastic move toward improving your game, practice this exercise. Once you get it, try it with your other hand.

Some tips on topspin: Remember that the more topspin you want to hit, the more you must get the racket head below the ball, take the ball "out in front," and swing "up" (not out) at the hit. Most pros who teach you to bend your knees and get "low" on groundstrokes haven't been watching what's going on out there among the players. John McEnroe, Michael Chang, Andre Agassi, and countless others all stand or jump when they whip their topspin forehands. If you want to put extreme topspin on the ball, then stand up at the hit; don't bend down. Bending is for flatter hits, such as the way Jimmy Connors plays. This allows your racket head to drop as far as possible below the ball. Then when you lift the edge up hard, it creates more spin, because it's moving faster and at a greater angle.

Forehands on the Run: The Sampras Style

The forehand on the run is one of the most beautiful and dynamic shots in the game of tennis. Pete Sampras just waits and prays for someone to pull him wide on his forehand. It's widely known, among real players, that this is one of Pete's premiere shots. The way he takes his racket back is designed for this shot.

Pete pulls his elbow back for his forehands, leaving his racket face close to the ball instead of laying the head back. In this way, he can hardly ever be "late" to the hit. His racket face is already facing the net and the court. He just goes through the middle of the stroke to the finish. He can go in either direction, cross-court or down the line. He usually chooses cross-court, which still catches most of his opponents off-guard because he hits so solidly. It's hard to believe that anyone can run in one direction and hit so hard in the opposite direction, but that's why he's one of the best who's ever played the game!

I've applied the above technique to my own forehand and to some of my students', and it really works. However, there is another way to hit this wide forehand on the run.

Borg's "Hook"

Most of the biggest topspin forehands are hit when players are on the run wide or short, and they have to pull the ball into the court. They let the tip of their racket drop to the ground, and then they sweep up the outside of the ball and hook it into the court. The first, and still most impressive, shot of this type that I ever saw was when I watched Bjorn Borg do it against a net-rushing John McEnroe back in the early '70s.

McEnroe came into net, as he usually did, and pulled Borg out wide, following his approach shot. McEnroe moved close to the net to cover both a down-the-line shot and a cross-court angle. Borg ran full speed, and while sliding on the clay, he dropped his racket head and hit the forehand toward the alley. He had thrown so much sidespin and topspin that you could see the ball curve in mid-air and eventually land at least a foot inside the sideline. Incredible shot! Borg used to let the head drop so much that when he hooked his arm around the ball, he could pull it cross-court, into the smallest court space imaginable. The ball took such a huge dip that he could hit the most amazing angles, too!

What Borg did, and many others do today, is let the head of their racket drop and come to the outside of the ball. Then, with a supple wrist, they pull the edge of the racket up the outside of the ball, creating topspin and sidespin, which pulls the ball toward the court. The keys are to: (a) Get the racket head under the ball ("on edge") by letting your wrist relax (pointing your fingers to the ground); (b) keep the face on edge and don't fold the racket face over during the hit (this will cause you to lose control of the ball); and (c) Just pull the edge up, and keep your weight moving to the outside of the ball; Don't move or pull away from the ball while you're hitting.

The more you drop the head, the more topspin you can create; the more to the outside of the ball you get, the more sideways curve you get.

There are two finishing points you can come to. You can either look under your arm, pulling the racket to the right side of your head, like Michael Chang does, or look over your arm, as you might on a flatter forehand. I like to look over my arm whenever possible. However, sometimes I find that it can be more effective and efficient to look *under* my arm. It can be a little dangerous to have that big racket head coming up toward your own head, so watch it!

With either finish, make sure to keep your hand loose, yet control your wrist. You want to bring the edge of the racket up on the outside of the ball, very cleanly. And you want to see it come up!

This method is different from Sampras's, in that the "hook" has more arch and more "dip," where Pete's has less angle, yet much more power. Both are awesome shots, and when applied with any degree of skill, they're worth having in your arsenal.

Open or Closed Stance?

Not too long ago, *Tennis* magazine came out with an article about wrong-footed forehands and how they could be a valuable asset to your game. They have been a major force since I've been playing. Top players such as Laver, Borg, Orantes, and Vilas used it; and now Agassi, Chang, and Sampras do. This shot is important! Everyone needs it. I strongly suggest that you add it to your repertoire.

Hitting off of the wrong foot (which for you righties, is the right foot) is a style that can work very well, especially if you're a back-court player. I have one junior boy student who uses the wrong foot exclusively, and quite successfully, on his Western (or closed-face) grip. His weapon includes: tremendous consistency, the ability to hit angles, a high-arching and quick-dipping ball path, and high bounces.

The beauty of the "open-stance," or "wrong-footed" forehand, is that it offers possibilities for self-expression. But I'll just tell you what I've found to be the basics:

You step somewhat parallel to the net with your right foot, or step away with your left foot. Your right knee bends, appropriate to the height of the ball, but in general, you do want to bend it. This "opens" your stance to the court. Now, because you don't have to step in with your left foot, you don't have to take as many steps to get in position to hit the ball. So it definitely economizes your footwork and energy. Also, you can get away with not having perfect footwork, because the stroke is more forgiving.

Also, you don't have to hit the ball so early, because you hit it more to the side rather than in front of you. That's why it's easier to disguise shots with a wrong-footed forehand—you can wait a little longer to swing.

The best open-stance forehands I've seen have started with the shoulders turned before the hit. Swing your nonhitting arm across your body, turning you sideways to the net, and bend your right knee. Your upper-body is "cranked" around, ready to unleash on the ball.

Step across with your right foot (open stance), and bend your knee. Extend your left hand while you bring your racket hand close to your body (use the backswing that works best for you).

The shoulders rotate into the contact, and the left arm swings open. The right knee straightens somewhat. You lift the racket-head edge up to your left shoulder. And as always, see the "spot"!

Shoulders rotate into the contact point; left arm swings open. Right knee straightens somewhat. You lift the racket head, edge up, to your left shoulder. Don't forget to see the "spot."

There are two ways of finishing that seem to work equally well, so do what feels good to you. You can either push up as you brush the face up the ball (remember to stay "on edge," using the straightening of your right leg for power), or you can just rotate your shoulders. Either way, remember to keep your eyes and racket head on the hit.

A good way to practice is to have someone (your coach) hit to you at the service line. Stand right at the "T," step across the service line with the wrong foot, then hit. Do everything the same with respect to seeing the "spot" and looking over your arm on the finish. Remember to start with your shoulders turned.

The Approach Shot

The forehand approach shot is one that requires the use of the wrong foot, and it is one of my favorite shots to show students. It's performed by nearly all great players, and there's a definite technique for learning it. But usually, a pro will just say something like, "Come on in on this one" or "Come on in down the line" (in singles). There is, however, a specific method that most good players apply, and it's really simple and feels natural with a little practice.

The best way to learn it is to go back to the service line and hit the wrong-footed forehand. Then immediately step toward the net on your left foot. That's it! Hit off the right foot, and continue to the net with your left.

On the move: Your left foot steps into the court. Your racket edge is continuing up, with your left arm swinging away. What finish does this look like?

This shot lets you hit while moving toward the net, at the same time keeping you sideways to the net throughout the stroke. Your first step actually "closes" you to the net. Just keep running or walking into net.

Inside-Out Forehands

The flatter you want to hit, the more you want to take the ball "on the rise" or at the top of its arch, and bring your fists and racket forward (rather than up, as for topspin). To hit a big flat forehand (the kind they call an "inside-out today"), just keep the racket face "on edge," and throw the tip of your racket to the top of the net, maintaining the integrity of the racket head "on edge." The shot comes from the shoulder, keeping the arm and racket on the same level. Make sure you throw the strings toward the top of the net.

I remember that the first time I saw this shot (executed perfectly) was at the Junior Nationals in Kalamazoo, Michigan, in 1973, when a great junior player named Horace Reid ran to the sideline, planted his right foot (the "wrong" foot), gave a glance cross-court, and then cracked this forehand down the line. He could "pass" players standing on the baseline; he was so quick that his ball traversed the court like a hockey slapshot! These days, I think that Jim Courier's the man to watch with this shot.

I've found that some players respond to being told to throw the tip ("on edge," of course) to the top of the net. This shot is not really an inside-out. It's more of a flat forehand. Try it. Remember, keep your arm and racket level, pretending you're dragging it along an imaginary table, and throw the tip forward. To hit the true inside-out forehand, just bring your grip through slightly before the racket head, causing your strings to contact the inside of the ball. Continue to throw your handle out toward the top of net.

Hitting a safer forehand just requires you to swing up at the ball. The more you swing straight forward, the harder you hit. The more you swing up, even on the high ball, the safer your shot is. Just don't wave the head of your racket at the ball, with the racket butt pointed down. The timing has to be too impeccable to make that shot. Bring your entire racket up to the same level (of the ball) if possible.

Return of Serve

Open-stance is generally a good shot for service returns, especially if the serve is coming too fast to get the left foot forward in good position. The best things to remember are: Start close to the middle of the stroke, preferably under the ball, and lift the racket face "on edge"—see the "spot"! Essentially, the stroke starts at the middle, but a proper finish will give you a harder and safer return.

Go right to the middle (the hit), from below the ball. Lift the edge.

Continue to lift the edge up clean, perpendicular to the court. No folding over! Eyes stay down on the hit.

◆ ◆ ◆

Maintaining fluidity on the forehand (and the two-handed backhand) is a matter of keeping the swing continuous. Your swing should remain smooth and even from the start through the finish. Don't slow down or speed up in the middle. Keep the speed constant. As you become more proficient, you can gradually speed up the stroke for a harder hit. Don't change the speed at the contact point, or the motion will become jerky, erratic, and uncomfortable.

Put some oil in your elbow—that is, let your arm relax, allowing your racket to drop under the ball naturally. If your finish seems stiff or forced, let your racket edge come up and touch your left shoulder, once again relaxing your elbow. That seems to help tight athletes look and feel smooth. Keeping it relaxed and flowing is what makes the forehand and the two-handed backhand feel so good, and what makes them so much fun to hit!

◆ ◆ ◆ ◆ ◆

Chapter Four

ALL THE BACKHANDS

The Two-Hander

We don't have to spend too much time on the two-handed back-hand, because it is virtually a left-handed forehand (righties), with a little help and guidance from the right hand.

The left hand is on top supplying the power, while the right hand controls the face of the racket, keeping it "on edge." (This is another good reason for hitting lefty in the warm-up.)

Grips are not that important on this shot, so long as your racket face stays flat to the net and under control. Jimmy Connors claimed that he never switched grips at all to hit his backhand. If your shots are "float-ing," or going long, you might want to move your grip (on your right hand) over to more of a full backhand grip (when your knuckles are on top of the grip, placing your racket face parallel with the net).

Review the forehand rules, and apply them to the two-handed back-hand, always remembering that the left side does most of the work—that is, the chin now presses against your left shoulder, and your left foot pivots.

The main thing to remember on the two-handed backhand *starting* point is to keep your hands close to your left hip pocket. That is, don't take your hands away from your body. (Remember the tennis ball in the armpit?)

Start on-balance. Turn your shoulders to the ball without dipping the front shoulder, which creates a bend from the waist. You want to be looking straight at the ball, not leaning over it. I've actually heard pros teach students to dip their right shoulder for power. That's wrong. You want to keep your chest lifted and your chin up.

Hands are close to the left hip pocket, elbows in. Shoulders are turned sideways to the net; the right foot steps forward.

Once again, make sure to drop your racket below the ball. If your backhand feels too much like a "push," then let the racket *head* drop more in the back. Let your fingers relax and point to the ground behind your left foot (dropping the head of the racket below the ball). Make sure to drop behind your left knee (or your ankle on low balls) so you can hit the ball with your racket face coming up. Yes, by dropping the head, you might use some wrist action, but if you stay "on edge," you'll keep the wrist under control, and it can make the stroke feel more relaxed and natural. It can also add power and topspin because you're using more leverage. Either start low or "loop" below the ball. If you're looping, keep the swing fluid. Don't stop at the bottom.

The *middle* is still the most important part of the stroke; make solid contact with a flat racket face on the way up. Review the "spot" drill. Once again, if you're have trouble making good contact, go to the "touch and finish" method.

Hands close together, eyes on contact point, pressing the ball against the net tape. Racket edge is parallel to the net, coming forward and up.

Finish, as on the forehand, by looking over your left arm, chin to your shoulder, with the racket head higher than your own head. A good technique to make sure that your eyes and weight stay on the hit is to look at the ground (where the ball was hit) after contact is made.

Pivot the back foot so you rotate your body weight into the hit, on-balance. Both knees should be facing forward. An alternate way to bring your weight forward and finish the stroke is to do what Jimmy Connors does. He picks his back foot up and swings it around to the outside of the ball, getting tremendous body weight into the ball. I feel the pivot is more stable, but do what feels right for you.

Finish: Racket head high, left elbow pointed forward, chin to shoulder. Roll back toe completely, to turn the body open to the net. Knees, hips, and shoulders are square to the net.

Often two-handers look stiff because the *finish* is straight out in front, making the stroke feel like a "push." Touching your shoulders with the edge of your racket will help keep your stroke relaxed and smooth, while adding topspin.

Alternate finish: Elbows collapse, and the racket edge touches your back. Don't turn it over; stay "on edge."

If you're having trouble staying on-balance, try stepping straight into the court (toward the net), even slightly open-faced. Bjorn Borg used to do this beautifully, disguising his shots. This makes it easier to pivot, shifting your body weight forward on-balance. You might also want to try keeping your chin up and your shoulders drawn back slightly throughout the swing. I've noticed that many club players lean forward from their shoulders, causing an uncomfortable swing, and often back pain. Notice Jill's posture in the finish: her torso is straight, shoulders level, and she's not leaning over the ball.

You might also want to try swinging your left foot around during the swing. Some players find that this gives them a more aggressive weight transfer and increased power. Ideally, you want your left hand and left hip to come forward, or rotate, together.

Finally, keep in mind that to hit an effective two-hander, you're going to have to anticipate where the ball is going, and move faster to get there than on a one-hander, because you lose about 30 percent of your reach. Additionally, you need to pivot the back foot, and it's easier, as we discussed, to stay on-balance if you're stepping forward (toe pointed toward the net) rather than across your body. (If you step across, your legs can get tangled during the pivot.)

The (Still) Classic One-Hander

Some claim that the one-handed backhand is the most natural and easy shot in tennis. Natural, physiologically, maybe, but not easy for everyone. The reason it is touted as "natural" is because, unlike the forehand, you don't need any real body action. Your hitting arm is in front of your body; therefore, there's no need to pivot. You could basically sit in a chair and hit a backhand, which would be awkward with the forehand because your arm's swing would be blocked by your body. As natural as it may be, many club players feel that they cannot get any power, fluidity, or confidence with this stroke. The reason is that most people don't do anything on that side of their body, or with the back of their hand. Although this will be an easy shot for you to learn, there are a few things you have to watch out for, or this shot can go awry.

First, make sure that your grip keeps the racket face flat to the net ("on edge"). You can do this by once again standing by the net and wedging the ball between your strings and the net, holding the ball there for a moment. Turn the grip until you can hold the ball in place comfortably, keeping the edge parallel with the net. Once again, roll the ball over the net. It's so important to understand this image and concept. It is the key to good groundstrokes.

Your backswing can be relatively simple. Use your left hand to pull the racket back to your left hip, as it also performs the job of changing the position of your hand to the continental (the one used for serves, volleys and overheads) or full backhand grip. The left hand should start placing the racket "on edge."

Step toward the net, right hand by your hip pocket, left hand holding the racket "on edge." The front knee is slightly bent, facing forward, arm slightly bowed.

Once again, you'll have to get your racket under the ball by relaxing your elbow and dropping your hand below your left sock. Make sure to drop the racket behind you and not on the way to the hit. The more you drop the handle and keep the head up, the flatter you'll hit the ball. The more you drop the head, the more topspin you'll get.

Then, as with the forehand, you'll want to hit the ball while the racket is on the way up from below the ball. Remember to keep your face "on edge" at all times.

Now, bring your racket head up to the "spot," rolling it over the net. Eyes down on contact, racket edge coming up, parallel to the net.

If you have trouble controlling the face, try sweeping the tip of the racket up and around the outside of the ball, especially if you're pulled wide. This often helps to keep the racket face from opening up.

Always "air out" the armpit completely—that is, let your arm and racket come up ("on edge") so that you make a "T"-shape with your body. Airing out the armpit will ensure a complete follow-through and a swing from the shoulder. The straighter your arm is, the better. Some players on the tour seem to throw their chest out as they split their hands. Try it. It's a good way to keep your torso level, keeping you on-balance.

Simultaneously while you're airing out your armpit, throw your left hand back toward the back fence. Finishing like a capital "T" can at first feel a little stiff, but it will help you stay sideways to the net, giving you a solid hit every time. What I notice players doing wrong some-times is that they throw their left hand up but not back toward the back fence. They open up and mishit off the top of their racket.

The simplest and still the best back-hand finish. Right side facing the net, arms straight, right armpit aired out completely. Back heel slightly lifted but not pivoted.

Be sure that when you finish, you're facing the side fence and not the net, eyes down (focusing on the point where the ball was hit). Unlike the forehand and two-fisted backhand, you want to stay closed, sideways to the net, on this shot. Opening up here will pull you off the ball. Split your arms symmetrically for better rhythm, balance, and tim-ing. One of my youngest students told me that it feels like you're going "Ta dah!" as you split your hands apart symmetrically (wisdom from the mouths of babes).

The Backhand Chip

There are two types of chips. The first kind are the "floaters," which sail up, bounce high with little or no forward momentum, and "sit up" like a meatball, ready to be devoured. The other "stings"; the ball skims low over the net, and upon hitting the court, it stays very low and skids quickly forward. This shot puts your opponent on the defense because it's hard to get the racket head below the ball, often causing him or her to hit into the net. The stinging, or biting, chip is tough to return. It's a great shot to use on high bouncing balls, approach shots, return of serve, when you're too tired to swing up for topspin, and when returning a good chip (because it's too difficult to get under and hit topspin).

A continental grip usually works better than a full backhand grip or any forehand grip because the face is naturally slightly open. It's really the best grip to hit the shot, although you can do it with the full backhand grip. Using a forehand grip will just float the ball.

To start, take the racket head back to your left side in a relaxed fashion, arm bowed. Some people go at this shot with an extremely bent elbow, looking like they're about to chop down a cherry tree. You want your arm at about a 45-degree bend. Start with your racket head slightly above the ball.

Racket head higher than handle, left hand pulls racket throat back across from left ear. Eyes and right shoulder are facing the ball.

For the middle portion of the chip, try to throw the tip of the racket toward the top of the net, going through the outside of the ball. Go cross-court at first because it *forces* you to get your racket head to the outside of the ball, rather than pushing your handle down the line. Once you get the hang of it, you can aim anywhere. The face can open gradually at the finish, making it look as if you were an umpire yelling "Safe!" At the contact, however, don't put the emphasis on opening the face, or else your ball will float. Personally, I find that if I hit my chips with a flatter face, they seem to stay lower and harder, with more "bite" (speed and skid). Opening the face is more for a drop shot, which we'll talk about later.

Contact point: tip of the racket to the "outside" of the ball, arm straight, face just slightly "open," head of the racket level with handle. Eyes on contact point.

A tip: You'll find that the best chips are hit more to the side (as shown in the above picture), when you can hold the ball on your strings. If you hit too far in front of you (without moving in, like on a "chip and charge"—described later on), you lose the ball immediately upon impact. This results in a weak shot—one that either "floats" up or drops in the net. I'm sure you've been told to hit all strokes "out in front of you," but that's not always true.

To finish: Thrust the racket toward the ball as if stabbing the final blow in a swordfight. Bring the head out at the ball with the entire racket. Do not let the head drag or you'll hit "floaty" high volleys, as well as hitting a lot of balls wide (because you'll be hitting the inside-bottom of the ball). Do not push your handle at the ball.

Left hand is outstretched behind you, with your side to the net. Racket head level, or slightly below handle, some-what open, tip forward. Eyes down at the contact point.

It's not really a "high-to-low" motion. It's actually more of a "high-to-middle" swing. The stroke starts higher than the ball, but at contact it levels off at about the height of the ball. It's not like chopping down a tree or chipping a golf ball. As you get to the "outside of the ball," the head naturally begins to level off.

The head of the racket will usually finish even with or slightly below the handle. You should experiment with the finish, but start by pointing the tip of the racket at the net post with your arm completely straight. Other players point the tip of their racket at the top of the net. Some coaches teach that the head should stay up, but this can become too much of a push. Others tell you to open the face as you swing. It will take forever to learn it that way. The ball will float. Your face only opens slightly, and if you have a continental grip (starting high and finishing low), that's enough underspin.

You need some headweight to give the shot some velocity and "bite." "On guard!" Stick that ball with the tip of your racket coming out like a sword, stabbing the top or the middle of the net. The more headweight you get, the more "sting" you get on the ball. That ball moves quickly and does not come up (off the bounce).

Approach: Chip and Charge!

Coming in off a backhand chip is known in the tennis world as "chip and charge," and it can be an effective play. The idea is to keep moving through the hit, just like on the forehand approach, not stopping at the hit. Unlike the forehand, you cannot hit this shot off the wrong foot because it's too difficult to get your front shoulder turned to the net, which is a must.

But like the forehand, you still want to stay sideways throughout the hit and first step. Cross-step the left foot behind the right as you contact the ball, as shown in the photo on the next pege. This allows you to stay sideways to the net, as you continue moving forward.

Cross-step behind to stay sideways while moving, ball out to side at contact; eyes down on contact point, left hand back.

The Chip Return of Serve

This is a vital shot for any player. It's your basic chip backhand. Turn your shoulders off of the split-step, step if you have time, and catch the "outside of the ball," especially against kick serves. Don't let that ball get away from you! Remember that all the rules of the chip apply. Swing high to level, get the head moving, and don't open the racket face too much.

Service Returns and Passing Shots, on Both Sides

The most important thing to remember when hitting your return of serve and your passing shots is to stay with the hit. Keep your weight solid on the ground, and don't pull your body or your eyes away. Stay put, with an open or closed stance. Hit the shot frozen, and then move to the next shot. Often, players try to get to the center of the court before they finish hitting their stroke. Other times they try to get into position while they're hitting. Forget it. Get in the best position possible before the ball bounces (on your side), and once it bounces, stay put.

Chapter Five

WIN AT NET

"**P**unch!" Now, there's a tennis concept for the history books. Ancient history. According to the tennis world, that concept is the key to life at net. But let me ask you something: Is that what it looks like when Stefan Edberg hits his volleys? Certainly that's not the volley Agassi uses when he hits his swinging topspin up at net, which happens to be a great and relatively simple shot (shown earlier in the forehand exercise for advanced players). Personally, I've never seen Andre miss one. Have you?

A "punch" reminds me of a "jab," something very abrupt and jerky looking. You've tried it. Does it look like you and Edberg are doing the same thing? I don't think so. His stroke looks different, because it *is* different!

There are some simple and effective techniques that can make your volleys feel natural and effortless, while at the same time making them crisp and consistent. Try to incorporate the following tips into your volleys, and see a major improvement! But the most important thing to remember is: Keep it simple!

◆ ◆ ◆

The Gist of It

Solid contact on volleys, more than any other stroke, is everything. The volley for the majority of players is 90 percent middle, with a small backswing and almost no finish.

Where you hit the ball in relation to your body, however, is crucial. The common mistake is to take the volley "too late" or too far in front of you. That's right—despite what you might think or what you've probably heard, the volley can be mistakenly taken too far in front of you. This can be just as detrimental to your volley as taking it too far behind you.

Habits to Live by at Net

Your preparation position is: hands out in front, right hand on the grip, left on the throat, knees bent, and eyes forward. Don't let your racket dangle to your side. This will slow down your reaction time immensely.

It's more important to stay low at the net than it is in the backcourt, primarily because things happen much quicker up there, and presumably you're not hitting topspin. Since you only have time for one step at net, make it an explosive one à la Becker (and his great gets).

Also, you want to stay low so you can view the ball coming at you, instead of looking on top of it. You'll soon see that it's best to bring your racket head forward or bring the bottom edge slightly down on most volleys, unlike the flat/topspin groundstrokes where you lift the racket and the ball up. You don't hit the ball with an arch at net (except, of course, on the swinging volley). The volley is basically the deflection of the ball off your strings.

Move as if you're in a dollhouse. Creep around up there, but try not to bend at the waist. Rarely do you get to run at net, unless, of course, you're running back to track down a lob. So don't stand flat-footed with your hands at your side. Your body at net should be very much alive.

"Touch-down," or split-step, at about the time your opponent makes contact with the ball. Keep your hands out in front of you, and quickly turn your shoulders immediately after the split. The touchdown is a hesitation move (to see which direction the ball is going off your opponent's strings, and to prepare for an explosive first step). Remember, you want a low, powerful move, so move from your navel. The "split and push off" movement is critical for an effective net game. We'll talk more about this later in the chapter called "Court Coverage."

As I mentioned earlier, it's best to volley with a continental grip, because then your grip stays the same for both forehand and backhand. Once you're at net, the ball comes too quickly to have the time to change grips. Additionally, the continental grip gives you a natural backspin on both sides, and it helps make low volleys easier because the face is slightly open. If you must, however, and you're quick enough, it's all right to switch grips, but not at the "A" or "Open" levels. No time for that.

See the hit! Control the face of your racket head, and see it meet the ball. Be painstakingly conscious of the angle of the racket head, and be deliberate about the hit. Don't just block it back. Remember that the face is the key. Maintain the attitude of the racket face to the ball and the net throughout the hit—no turning it open or closed during the stroke.

Once you have a good "feel" for your racket head up at net, you can then begin to squeeze the racket handle upon impact with the ball, banging the head of the racket slightly forward. This gives the volley just a little more zip off your strings. To hit with more power, bang it forward; to hit more underspin, bring the bottom edge slightly down, as if you were tapping a nail into the court.

Practice your racket-face control by holding your racket still at the moment of contact with the ball. This will help you to notice the hit more, as well as maintain control over the racket head. This is also a good exercise to allow you to see how your face was angled and where the head was at impact point.

◆　◆　◆

The *approach volley,* as I call it, is the one that you use as you're running to the net, and it's usually hit at about the service line and even beyond. Use this volley when you're forced to hit on the run, which is different from the volley you'd use when you're situated close to the net. That one is best hit with your feet stationary.

This volley requires that you control the face of your racket (and your arm) while moving. Unlike the close-to-the-net volley, where you're standing still, the approach volley is hit with almost no wrist action or headweight at all. Run with the racket to your side whenever possible, and just hold it there steady as if you're dragging the head of your racket through water; the racket head stays to the side or even slightly behind the handle, and you just "walk through" the hit. On that volley, the most important thing is that you deflect the ball deep into the court, setting you up for the more aggressive net play that will follow. The only arm movement you might make is reaching your hand slowly to the baseline.

The Forehand Volley Winner

Get your left hand across your body to help turn your left side to the net and to get some shoulder strength behind the hit. Stabilize your left shoulder. Most players have trouble with the forehand volleys, especially the "easy" ones, because they rotate their shoulders during the hit, opening up to the net. This creates an instability in the stroke, resulting in mishits, mistakes, and an overall lack of confidence. Throw a dart, and you'll see that your entire body is stabilized except for your throwing arm. Your shoulders don't move.

I know that you've probably been taught to "turn sideways" on your volleys, but that piece of instruction is not quite enough. Some volleys you have to turn more on than others. Stabilizing your left shoulder is what's really important. The following exercise is useful to really understand the shoulder's job:

Grab the net with your non-hitting hand, with your left shoulder across your body. Now have someone feed balls to your forehand, and volley them back, leaving your hand on the net (and your shoulder in place).

Then, bring your hitting hand out to the side, elbow slightly bent and pointed down for the duration of the short swing. Bring your forearm out into the court, leaving it and the palm of your hand facing the net throughout. Keep your elbow in and comfortably bent at your side, like you're about to throw dice on a craps table.

Forehand Volley Exercise: Grab the net with your left hand (to stablilize your left shoulder). Lay the racket back slowly, and as you hit the ball, lock the head forward and stop.

During the entire stroke, you want to make sure that you keep the head of the racket slightly above the handle, except for the very lowest volleys, when the head will have to drop even lower than the handle. If the head is too high, with the racket butt pointed down, you'll tend to flop the head over and down, hitting short, or in the net. Lay the racket off to the side almost even with the handle, head just slightly higher, but make sure the top of your racket faces the side fence.

Warning: Don't drive yourself crazy trying to keep the racket head "up," or keeping your human face close to the racket face. Those are some common volley cliches that don't hold up in a game.

I had a coach that made me try to see the ball coming through the strings, always screaming at me, "Both heads up, both butts down." I went through the juniors having "nothing volleys"; no one could pass me, but I couldn't put them away! Then I started watching the great juniors at the time: Perry Wright, Matt Mitchell, Ferdi Taygan, and John McEnroe. They all looked so comfortable and smooth when they hit their volleys. They would let the ball fall almost directly to their side (looking pretty relaxed and easy) instead of trying to "take it out in front" as much as they could, as I had always done. Not only did they look better, their volleys were all deep and deadly. I changed to a better volley.

Shake your racket head gently at the ball, as if you're shaking the salt out of a salt shaker, pretending that the corn cob is the net. It takes a supple wrist to lay the racket back slightly and bang it forward, locking it in at the contact point.

Once again, the left shoulder remains stablized, while the racket head is locked into place on contact.

You can also try cupping your hand around the ball. Make sure to start with a fairly loose wrist and squeeze it into place, parallel to the net, with your hand and racket face open to the net. Don't get too loose or you'll end up swinging at the ball with a wild wrist.

Stop on contact! Hold your racket gently while you lay the head back, then squeeze your fingers at the contact point, and stop. This gets the head of your racket banging out a little more at the contact point. This also helps to lock your wrist firm on contact.

When in doubt, go cross-court with the volley. Cross-court is generally going to be your strongest and most solid volley. Why? Because when going cross-court, you'll try to hit more of the outside of the ball, bringing the head around faster at impact point, hitting the ball with greater leverage and headweight.

Stop immediately upon contact (again)! This is the surest way to keep your wrist firm and your racket face under control. Also, this is an excellent method to check yourself, your balance, your distance from the ball, and your racket head position—basically, you're "freezing your finish."

Stay solid at the net. When you've finished the stroke, you should still be facing the right sideline fence. There's no pivot, follow through, or "opening up" on the volley, as there is on the forehand groundstroke. Feet stay flat and solid on the ground. Moving is unnecessary. and usually detrimental to the success of the stroke. Even when you're charging, or making a diving get, your body stays in control. If you have trouble staying closed, try either grabbing your right shoulder with your left hand (and volley), or criss-cross your left arm over the top of your right one throughout the stroke. This is *not* a low overhead.

Some coaches are really concerned with the amount of backspin you get on the ball because that's what we were all taught 20 years ago. The rackets at that time had no power, so you had to hit with a lot of underspin to keep the ball low (especially on grass or clay) so they wouldn't pass you on the next shot. Hate to say it, folks, but look around. The rackets are bigger, longer, and more powerful today. Points at net don't last that long anymore, especially on hard courts. Just watch Sampras against Ivanisevic.

High Forehand Volleys

The only real difference on the high forehand is that the racket head must be a little higher than the handle, and you shouldn't use any wrist. The key is to avoid just pointing the head up, with the racket in a vertical position. When that happens, people tend to wave the head at the ball with a loose wrist, mishitting the ball short.

Lift your racket handle, as well as the head. Try to keep the racket as horizontal as you can, and push the handle forward with a firm wrist. Push the racket to the ball as if you were pushing a wall at it. No wrist action (or very little), please!

Left hand up and across; right hand lifted, level with shoulder.
Push handle forward. Nothing fancy.

Backhand Volleys That Sting

Hands start out in front, right hand on the grip, left on the throat; have your left hand bring the racket head toward the ball. Because the ball is to your left, find the ball with your left hand. This is the easiest and most efficient way to locate and hit the ball. Experiment: Throw a ball to the left side of someone's body and yell, "Catch!" Which hand does he or she use to catch it? You'll find that the left hand finds the ball.

"Push" the right hand to the side of you as the back of your right shoulder faces the net. Lay the racket head back slightly if you want more power. Like the forehand, you're going to flick the head of your racket at the ball, now locking your wrist and arm straight (and leaving it straight) on contact.

Back of shoulder pointed at ball; sideways to net; right foot forward.
Right hand pushed to the side and away from body; left hand hold-
ing racket throat back, "face" slightly open, higher than handle.

Don't bend your arm and pull the racket behind your left ear. That is where most people go astray. There should be a slight bow in your hitting arm. The less elbow you use in this shot, the less chance of error. When you bend your elbow, you take the racket head way too far away from the middle, or contact point. You end up being late a lot, especially when you're under pressure. I found that when I was a Junior and started with a bent elbow, I never had any confidence, not even on the easy volleys.

Once your arm is fairly straight and parallel to the net, you use your shoulder, bringing the back of your arm to the net (something my college coach told me). At the same time, squeeze your fingers and lock the wrist, which will bang the racket head forward. This volley is safe, reliable, and it stings. I learne this one primarily from watching John McEnroe, who probably had the best backhand volley of all time! However, I've noticed that all the great volleyers straighten their elbow on contact.

Lock the wrist on contact, banging the head out slightly first. Racket face forward, arm straight. Throw left hand up and back to stay sideways. Certainly you've noticed that most people back-hand-volley better when they're pulled wide.

As with the forehand, try to keep the head of the racket slightly above the handle whenever possible on medium to high volleys. Snap that racket head forward, and stop at contact, with a straight arm. Try not to let your racket head come across your body, or "chop" down. Just making good contact with a continental grip provides ample power and spin.

As with the forehand volley, if you want to get a little more power on the ball, don't swing harder. Simply try to squeeze your fingers gently, and bang your racket head to the outside of the ball and stop. You'll find that here, too, most of your best volleys go cross-court, given the additional headweight.

High Backhand Volleys

Now here's an interesting shot that is rarely dealt with by club players or their pros. It is a unique shot—one that turns a player into a tennis master.

The backhand volley is hit with your shoulder to the ball, while the high backhand volley is hit with your back to the ball. You can follow a general rule: The higher the volley, the bigger the turn; the lower the volley, the less you turn. The high backhand volley is hit by making your body a human "wall" back to the hit.

How it works is, after you split, you point your back to the net, peering over your shoulder to see the oncoming ball. Of course you won't be able to step forward. You'll have to step to the side fence. Your racket is pulled to the left side of your body, slightly bent.

Pull your racket back with your left hand; pointing your back into the court. Step to the sideline.

Then, strike the ball by locking your two arms straight so that there's a straight line from one hand to the other, making you parallel to the net, body facing the back fence. It's a quick, strong move. Maintain your solid-wall stance; don't let the racket head and your wrist flip over. Keep your back to the net, and your eyes up on the contact point.

Contact with both arms straight, like a wall; back facing net, parallel. Eyes up on contact.

Two-Handed Backhand Volleys

Well, all I've got to say on this one is: Learn to hit a one-hander!

The Ball Coming at You

When a ball is hit directly at your body, I would suggest, in most cases, to take it as a backhand volley. Draw your left shoulder back as you bring your right shoulder to the net, and then straighten your arm as you contact the ball. The back of your arm still faces the net, with your right shoulder turned to the net. Every ball is essentially a wide volley. React quickly. Get your arm straight! Lean back with your shoulders, but stay on-balance.

Solid Overheads: "Back of the Ball"

What you may have heard in the past: "Toss higher, jump, scratch your back with the racket, and snap your wrist." Right? I don't think so. The majority of players who follow this instruction do not have a reliable overhead. *My* advice is: "Scratch your head, hit the back of the ball, throw your edges, and create headweight."

Most players below 5.0 (advanced) try to swing down on their overheads and on their flat, hard serves, especially after they've been told their entire life to "snap the wrist." At best, they mishit off the top of their racket, causing a short or weak hit; at worst, they miss the ball completely, sometimes hitting their racket against their chin. I wish I were kidding (that looks like it hurts).

Hit the "back of the ball." This is the part of the ball that's directly facing the fence behind you. It's not necessary to swing too hard. Just reach up and bump it; make contact! The head traveling from below your shoulder blades up to the ball is enough leverage to hit the ball with good velocity. Just touch the back of the ball—not the bottom, not the side, not even on top—but the very back of the ball.

Tip (top) of the racket is straight up, eyes up; touching the very "back of the ball."

You'll be surprised what this technique can do for your overheads and flat serves. Even just reaching up gradually will produce a surprisingly hard, deep, and consistent overhead. Practice by hitting 20 in a row. It shouldn't be difficult if you can maintain the focus on your contact point, which is the back of the ball. Be committed to this concept. It will win matches for you! It's so vital to your flat serves and overheads that I've already mentioned it five times!

Positioning Makes the Overhead Do-Able

Turn sideways to the net the moment you see the lob go up. Your hitting hand goes immediately behind your head to get your elbow bent and poised for the swing, as your left hand goes up to gauge the distance of the ball, making sure it doesn't get behind you, or to your left.

Left hand pointed up, arm straight; body sideways to the net. Right hand behind your head, elbow bent; eyes up.

The left hand is also up to judge depth. It's awfully hard to tell if the ball is 10 or 13 feet high without some reference point, which this hand serves as. Some players like to point the tip of their racket at the ball; others just drop the racket head down their back. Either one is okay.

Swing up to the back of the ball. Straighten your arm at the hit; get all the momentum and leverage you can. Big overheads are hit with momentum, not muscle. Pivot your back foot during the swing to rotate your body into the hit and stay on-balance. Your left hand will naturally drop to your side or bend across your chest.

Arm straight, racket face bumping the back of the ball. Back foot is pivoted. Eyes up.

Once you've hit the ball, continue to leave your eyes up (past the hit). This helps deter you from pulling your head down before the hit. Probably the number-one reason for missing overheads is that you pull your head down just before the hit, causing you to hit in the net, shanking off the frame or missing altogether!

Your finish should be slow and controlled. You should not hear a "whiffing" sound. Remember, it's not the speed after the hit that matters; it's the speed going *to* the hit. Most players pull too hard down, taking their eyes, weight, and racket head with them. This usually results in a mishit off the top of the racket. Basically, momentum and gravity bring the racket down most naturally.

It's probably best for players to hit their overheads (especially in practice) down the line. This is naturally your most solid and consistent overhead under pressure. I say "under pressure" because most people have no trouble with the overhead until the pressure is on. When players get nervous, they tighten up and have a tendency to open up to the court too early and hit wide. Therefore, by practicing overheads down the line, you'll at least keep the ball in play when you get nervous. It's also your hardest and flattest overhead because when most people hit cross-court, they slice (taking pace off the ball). Additionally, it goes to a righty's backhand. Hit 90 percent of your overheads down the line, and this shot will become more of a weapon for you.

◆　◆　◆　◆　◆

Chapter Six

SERVES YOU CAN COUNT ON

The serve is a very personal and individual aspect of the game. There are as many different styles of serves as there are people. As such, I won't be a hypocrite and try to teach you the serve from a book. Your style is your own. However, it's important to keep in mind that there are certain fundamentals and principles that can help all serves.

Flat Serves

No, you're not supposed to "snap your wrist"—that's what the other guys (and ladies) teach. In actuality, you're supposed to snap your wrist (naturally); you're just not supposed to focus on it. Speaking of which, have you ever asked your instructor exactly where, when, and how hard you're supposed to "snap it"? I think the answer would be: "Hit several hundred buckets of balls, and they'll start to fall in." (Yeah, right. Like pennies from heaven.) In fact, there *are* some concrete fundamentals that make serves work.

Your serve won't necessarily get powerful if you "use your legs" or "rock." You need to practice these serves continually, or else these instructions just throw your timing off. But don't despair. There *is* a way to hit big serves with dependability. Remember, it's not the style that puts the ball in. It's contact. Surround the contact with your own style, one that feels good to you. Once you know how and where to make the best contact, you can use any style, and even several different ones.

What will give you a consistent, flat serve is your ability to toss to your right, cock your hand behind your head, and focus on contacting the back of the ball. That's it. But here's a good tip: Make sure your grip doesn't slip in your hand, back to a forehand. This will cause you to hit the inside of the ball, sending it long and wide. A way to stop changing the grip (during the stroke) is to hold the racket in the continental grip loosely until the hit.

Hit Big: Create Headweight

Throw the head of your racket at the ball. Create leverage. Hit the ball as if you were hammering a nail, as if you're throwing your racket head at the ball. However, as reckless as I want you to be with the racket head, make sure you see it hit the back of the ball, *head first.*

Good practice: Find a field (or a golf course), and throw your racket as high and hard as you can. Do this a few times, really feeling the weight build in the head. On the court, you can try this: Pretend the head of your racket weighs 50 pounds, and that the rest of it weighs only one pound. Throw it like you would hurl a sack of potatoes. Headweight is accountable for at least 80 percent of your serve's power and spin, and it makes more sense than snapping your wrist. The more weight you can create in the head, the harder you can serve. You don't even have to be particularly strong to hit it hard.

The "Sundial Method" for Spin

The conventional serving methods don't work well, primarily because it takes too long to make them work. Serving is more than applying a few stylistic feats and then relying on finding a "feel" for it. You might groove a service motion, but that doesn't necessarily mean you'll be able to hit the serve you want when you need it. What if you're too nervous to feel, or your feel is a little off? Remember: It's not style that puts the ball in the court; it's contact.

The best I've ever served in my life, to this point, was my last year at U.C. San Diego. I was serving impeccably—big, flat serves down the middle; heavy, wide slices and kicks pulling players off the court. My first serve was probably 106 m.p.h., and probably 65 percent of them were going in! (These were with wood rackets.) My doubles partner, Billy, told me to keep serving second serves, because the spins were just as difficult to return as the flat ones (maybe more). I was obviously fully focused on the ball, and I had lots of confidence.

That's when I decided that it was a good time to figure out what it is that makes these serves go in, and go in so well. Your serve has to be there all the time! I tried to think of what it looked and felt like while I was hitting these big serves. I felt my legs bend and push up; I heard myself inhale with the wind up, and exhale with the hit. For spins, I saw different edges of my racket head fly up to and past the ball; and for flat serves, I saw the face hit the back of the ball. It felt as though my racket was a hammer, and the different edges would be used to hit the nail, either in a wall (slice) or a ceiling (topspin).

The method that I created is *The Sundial,* and it never fails—I guarantee it! Yes, you too can hit a big-spin second serve—even under pressure—and have it go in!

A continental to full backhand grip works best for both slice and topspin serves. Stay away from the Eastern grip (the "handshake grip"—the one that keeps the racket face parallel to the net on the forehand side) or the Western (or closed-face) forehand grip. When you hold your racket to serve, hold it "on edge," with the "U" of your index finger and thumb on top, facing you.

◆　◆　◆

Start with the premise that if you hit a flat serve, your face hits the back of the ball, and the tip (top) of your racket then points straight up. You can think of this as throwing the tip straight forward.

Now slide down the racket to one of the edges on the head—pick one. Use that edge as a hammer head. The edges of the racket produce different spins that go in by either hammering it forward (for slice), or up for topspin. The lower on the racket you go—that is, the farther toward the throat—the more spin you put on the ball.

Slice Serves

Here's how you use the slice: Look at your racket and pick out an edge, just below the top, maybe two inches down. Now, as you go to hit that flat-serve toss, throw that edge out at a wall in front of the ball.

Throw the (hammer) edge at an imaginary wall, head first, hitting the outside of the ball. Eyes, shoulders, and hips are facing ball. Always remember that "head first" produces "headweight."

That's slice—hitting the right side of the ball, causing it to move in the air from right to left, taking some pace off the ball. The more slice you want, the lower on the racket you go. Simple. It's an easy feeling and procedure to reproduce.

The ball toss is crucial, though. Simply put, you can't hit what you can't see. For slice and flat serves, you use the back of the ball as your target. Therefore, toss to your right, comfortably in front of you; it's easiest to see that part of the ball.

Righties, toss slightly to the right and in front of base-line. For flat and slice serves, tossing with the arm straight, palm open. The hitting arm is bent, the racket down the back, the hand is behind the head, and the eyes are up.

This produces a right-to-left spin, which moves the ball down as it moves to the right once you've cleared the net (by throwing the edge forward, almost up). McEnroe and Sampras probably hit two of the best slice serves. Mac would practically throw the side edge of his racket up and out, his ball pulling you right off the court.

Topspin/"Kick" Serves

This is probably the safest second serve to use when you're under pressure. It's safe, but it does move around a lot, and if done well, it can produce a big kick up and to the right. The beauty is, the more game pressure you feel, the harder you swing. I always served best under pressure because I would swing harder and harder. So when I was "choking," I would not only get the serve in with consistency, but the serve actually became more difficult to return due to all of all its movement. Now that's the way to choke. Topspin serves, like topspin groundies, go high over the net and come down abruptly, bouncing or "kicking" high upon landing.

These serves are simple. Take that same lower edge, and use it as your hammer. Throw it straight up to the sky, head first. Throw it hard. The strings will brush up the back of the ball, producing a forward spin or topspin. The lower the edge, the more spin. Eventually, when you get toward the throat of the racket, you'll hit the inside of the ball, producing a kick to the right.

Topspin serve: The toss is over, or behind, the head, depending on the amount of spin; knees bent. Throw the edge to an imaginary ceiling. Eyes up.

You'll have to bring the toss over your head, instead of to the right. Hammer that edge up into the ceiling. You want a tougher spin, a bigger kick. For even more safety, toss more to your left, allowing you to throw the bottom edge up.

Toss is farther overhead, even to your left, for a big kick, tossing arm straight up. Knees bent, right hand behind head, eyes up at the ball.

Throw the lower edge straight up into the ceiling, harder. Toss farther over your head, and throw that little piece of the racket frame up as hard and loose as you can. Stay sideways, or your edge will come around and forward, causing slice. The serve will probably still go in, but you'll lose the "kick." Staying sideways helps force your strings to spin the ball from left to right, and then up. That edge going up is what makes the ball spin in once you've cleared the net (by throwing it up hard). Staying sideways, causing the ball to rotate from left to right, makes the ball "kick" to the right.

If you have a strong stomach and back (and strong knees), you can toss far enough over your head to throw the bottom edge up and get a huge American twist. The "twist" is a dramatic (and beautiful) serve, whereby you toss far to the left, bending your knees and back in preparation for the hit. You can then hit an extreme topspin, causing the ball to bounce severely up and to the right. If you can do it (without hurting your back), it's a great serve to throw off your opponent. It's also a good serve to follow into net, because the high bounce gives you time to get close to the net before the returner hits it.

Service Motion Checkpoints
(Remember: styles are variable.)

Service preparation: Start loose from start to finish. Let the racket dangle before you start your wind-up. (This technique was first made famous by the Aussies.) Or, let the racket swing past your leg, holding it loosely in your fingers, à la Sampras. Whatever you do, don't "death-grip" the racket. This will tighten your arm and elbow to the point that you'll have less pace and a weary arm. Also, try keeping your face and neck muscles relaxed throughout the serve. Maintain a calm expression.

Get your focus geared up. Bounce the ball a few times. Look at your opponent, the court, and visualize the coming point (or at least the serve). Every serve deserves your undivided attention.

Hold the racket low on the grip, in your palm. You can even let your little finger come off the end of the grip. This helps you feel the head-weight of the racket and keeps your wrist and arm loose. Let the racket do the work! Derive power from the racket leverage and momentum, instead of from muscle. *Try serving with that finger off the grip. You'll see that you don't have to swing hard to hit hard.*

The Middle (or Wind-Up)

Symmetry helps to maintain a steady service motion, although it's not necessary—certainly not for Roscoe Tanner or Goran Ivanisevic, two of the greatest servers of all time. Start with your hands together at about your waist. Let your left hand (righties) hold the racket head to feel the natural headweight. Hold the ball with your thumb and first two or three fingers, and your racket throat with the remaining finger(s). Don't hold the ball in your palm; it can hurt your toss. Bring your hands down together, up together (making a "U" shape with your arms); bring your hitting hand behind your head, and then go up to the hit. For most players, it's easier to find the rhythm the more symmetrically your arms move. However, this is not essential to a good serve.

The tossing hand is extremely important. Lower that arm until the back of the hand hits the left leg (righties), at which point your arm will be straight and supinated (opening your palm to the sky). Keep it straight while you lift it up slowly and steadily. Don't flip or throw the ball with a knee-jerk reaction. Keep the speed of your tossing arm (and hitting arm) constant and relatively slow throughout the toss (and wind-up). Be careful not to turn your hand over or break your wrist at any point during the toss. It's not a throw; it's more of a "lift." Let go of all of your fingers at once, or else the ball will come rolling off and be erratic.

Your hitting hand must get behind your head to get the racket head down your back and get you poised for the hit. If you don't get your arm and racket in this position before you hit, you won't have any power or "snap." You'll end up "pushing" or "muscling" the ball with no leverage or headweight.

Make sure, however, to perform the entire service motion without stopping. Many players develop a "hitch" because they stop with their hitting hand behind their head and rest the racket on their shoulder. However, keep the racket head moving to keep the momentum going. Think about it. If you're going to stop at your shoulder and then start the hit again, you might as well just start in that position. The wind-up is just a waste of motion. (As a matter of fact, Chris Evert got to the quarterfinals of her first U.S. Open (when she was 16) starting the serve with her racket down her back.)

Focus on Contact

The most important part of every stroke is the middle—the contact point of the ball. The serve is no exception. Always remember that no matter what style of serve you have, the actual hit and power comes from the extension of your arm from a bent position. So, straighten your arm on contact!

Keep your eyes up, and try to see the actual hit. In fact, it's best to keep your eyes up past the contact point. Most players will tighten up and pull their racket head and their own head down, causing either a serve to go into the net or mishit off the top of their racket.

Rotate the shoulders into the hit, for flat and slice. It helps to think of replacing the left shoulder with the right one for power. Also, you can try pivoting the back foot or springing up into the hit by using your legs to bend and push up at the hit. These hints are more for style. One of the best ways to discover the right style for you is to watch the pros on TV and then try to imitate them.

The Finish

The finish of the stroke is variable. Some players follow through on their left side (crossing over their body). Others pull their arm off to the other side of their body (right for righties). It really should be what's most natural and comfortable for you. Experiment. I find that for myself and several touring pros (Sampras, for example), following through on the left works best for slice and flat serves, and finishing to the "outside" of my right leg works best for the topspin and "kick" serves.

One more tip (actually this is more like a trick): If you want your serve to go up the middle on the deuce court and wide on the ad side, leave your tossing hand up longer. This will keep your body sideways for a longer time, forcing you not to hit cross-court (to a righty's forehand).

Perfect Practice Makes Perfect

What you want to do is make your swing effortless and rhythmic. I make my best players serve blindfolded, just to see how "grooved" their swing is. Hit buckets of serves, and always make sure to aim at targets. You'll gain the confidence to swing naturally and to focus on the contact point, which is vital for the execution of a good serve. (In fact, that's a winning combination for all of the strokes!) Once you have the grooved stroke and can maintain your focus, your practice time can drop off, and you'll still have regular success with your serve.

Serve to both sides when preparing for a match. Most players will hit over 100 groundstrokes to warm up for a match, but when it comes to their serve, they'll hit only four or five to the deuce court. Your serve is just as important to the ad court.

Style: The Myth

Find a style that you feel comfortable with, one you like to perform. Once you've decided on a service motion, stick to it! Groove it. Make it yours. I can't tell you how many times a year I changed my service motion when I was a junior. I didn't know if I had a McEnroe serve or one like Roscoe Tanner. "Jump serves," "rocking," "open-stance"—it's not that important. Have you noticed that no two pros have the same service motion? What matters is what feels good to you, what's easiest to reproduce. Don't agonize over whether you need to lift your front toe when you rock. It doesn't really matter.

It's the fundamentals such as "headweight," "back of the ball," and the "sundial method" that make the serve work. That's what you need to understand and focus on. The rest is merely style, the icing on the cake. Don't get obsessive about it. Just pick one. Once you have your serve wired, you can add motion (for power), without losing any control or consistency.

An exercise that I've always done, and that my students continue to do in order to improve, is to serve while kneeling on the ground. It keeps you from pulling your eyes and head down, and it also forces you to swing up to the ball. I have students, myself included, that can consistently serve from the knees at over 50 m.p.h.! Style is just style.

◆ ◆ ◆ ◆ ◆

Chapter Seven

COURT COVERAGE

Early Preparation

Early preparation is not only the key to better shots, but it's a major part of your focus and attitude. Early preparation, just like relaxation and concentration, is a mindset and a cornerstone of a strong backcourt game. It is early preparation that leads to better timing, rhythm, and appropriate responsiveness. The difference between getting to the ball "on time" and "being early" is the difference between mediocrity and "winning at tennis." When you get to the ball early, you can set up properly. Early preparation allows you to be in a relaxed and controllable position so you can transfer your weight during the hit and finish your swing on balance. In essence, it puts you in the right place at the right time. When you've prepared early, you can set up properly for your best stroke.

Essential to early preparation is reacting to the ball at the point of impact off your opponent's racket. By getting there early, you are poised to make your best shot. When you're ready and focused, you can develop efficient timing.

The essence of early preparation is the concept of beating the ball to the bounce on groundstrokes. By doing so, you're in position before the ball is; and believe me, it's easier to hit when you're standing still.

Example: Let's say you're playing baseball, you're on deck, and the batter has just struck out. (The rules in this game, however, are such that once the batter steps away from the plate, the pitcher can pitch the next ball even if you're not in the batter's box.) So you have a choice: Either slowly jog or walk to the plate so you take your swing while you're stepping in the box, or hustle over to the plate so that when the pitch is delivered, you're standing there waiting, and you can just hit the ball. I mean, it's tough enough to hit a moving sphere with a moving bat (or racket). You only make things more difficult when you add a third moving entity—namely, your *body*.

The Benefits of Early Preparation

◆ Makes the stroke easier to hit
◆ Helps you maintain your rhythm, balance, and timing
◆ Enables you to dictate the pace
◆ Saves your arm
◆ Utilizes your energy

Recently, I was giving a lesson to Claire, a former college and tournament player who hadn't played for about six or seven years. She was trying to get back into tennis and thought she would hit against the ball machine and take lessons before playing with other people. We hit for ten minutes to look at her game. Her arm movements were fluid and seemingly had control. Her strokes and the pace of her shots seemed reasonably good, but there was something off about her game. She missed shots with regularity, and on other shots she looked off-balance and out of "sync," whether at the net or in the backcourt. She would look good for a few shots then hit one off the fence, then one into the net, and then she'd hit one long. It was almost as if she were a beginner. All the while, Claire was getting more and more frustrated and less and less confident.

Anything Claire had to move for, she couldn't handle. In essence, what I told her was that she was out of position, and therefore uncomfortable and strained when hitting the ball. Her beautiful strokes disappeared when she was stretched out and off-balance.

"Claire, try hitting for the next few minutes, and make sure your last step (before hitting the ball) is toward the net. That is, get over to the ball before it bounces, and then step forward into the court." She followed my instructions, and what a difference we noticed—almost immediately!

From that moment on, Claire looked more comfortable, and her stroke looked consistent, fluid, and effortless. She started to develop "court sense"—that is, she moved quicker without expending any additional energy. Her mistakes became less frequent, and she started looking somewhat under control. Claire was beginning to feel stronger, looking more relaxed and on-balance. You see, early preparation allows you to feel comfortable—in control of your body and, therefore, your game.

Weight distribution, proper finishes, and balance all hinge upon early preparation. The key to early preparation is that your take the ball in your comfortable hitting zone. It also allows you to get a good look at the ball, much like a professional basketball player might get a good look at the basket right before he lets loose with his shot. Early preparation gives you that crucial split second to set up.

Keys to Backcourt Movement

1. *Stay light on your feet.* Get ready to anticipate and react to the hit. Begin by getting alert and loose. Bounce from side to side lightly while staying on the balls of your feet, off your heels. Stay in motion in between the hits. Hold the racket loosely and comfortably out in front of you with the dominant hand on the grip. The other hand should either hold the throat or, if you use a two-hander, hold that hand above the dominant hand, also on the grip. Your eyes need to be looking ahead at the ball about to be struck by your opponent or your practice partner. You're going to want to move and get into position the moment the ball is hit.

2. *React to the hit by split-stepping* (to be discussed at length later in this chapter). The properly timed split step helps you to "push off" quickly in any direction. Both in the backcourt and at net, you can immediately push forward after a "floater" volley or short ball, back-pedal for an overhead, dive to the side to stop a passing shot, or run down a wide ball going for a passing shot. Getting your legs sufficiently flexed on the split helps you to quickly dodge balls hit right at you.

   Once the ball is hit, you need to race the ball into position. When I say "race the ball," I mean try to actually get into your best position *before* the ball bounces. Beating the ball to the bounce is the key. Use your speed as if you were in a sprint, taking whatever size steps are necessary to get there before the ball does.

4. *Keep moving until the ball hits the court.* Don't plant your feet too early! Remember, you're going to want to keep moving until the ball hits the ground. Stay light on your feet, and keep fine-tuning your position. Even when the ball is popped up and you're in position early, remain in motion by keeping your feet moving up and down (stutter-stepping) while the ball is headed for the bounce. Anything can happen: wind, spin, or a slight misjudgment on your part.

6. *Hit and recover.* Get ready to react to the ball with anticipation. After your stroke, quickly and lightly "bounce" back toward a center position. Recovery should be thought of as part of your preparation routine. The shot is not over until you move back to your ready position, anticipating the next shot, ready to react to the hit.

"All-Court" Footwork

Footwork is the foundation for a solid game. Proper footwork, from split-stepping to stutter-stepping (that is, running in place using tiny hummingbird steps), gives you the tools to execute early preparation, and makes the job of hitting the ball effortless. Solid footwork can transform an average "B" player into a solid "A," a competitive tournament player. It's not just important that you *get* from level "A" to level "B, though." It's also crucial *how* you do it.

Mastering your footwork can not only get you prepared for the ball early, but it is crucial for your development of rhythm, balance, and timing. In turn, sound footwork will enable you to play with more power, control, and consistency.

The key to good footwork is to keep in mind that *you* are the one who plays the ball. Don't let the ball play *you*. Proper footwork gives you the necessary dance steps to get to and from the ball gracefully and effectively. Good footwork can put you "in control" of your game. It's next to impossible to raise your level of tennis to its full potential unless you understand and practice the art of proper footwork.

The Benefits of Sound Footwork

◆ Keeps you in control of your stroke throughout the point

◆ Enhances your responsiveness and anticipation on the court

◆ Helps make your stroke more natural, effortless, and efficient

◆ Inspires and invigorates you while you're playing

◆ Gets you around the court more quickly and more efficiently

◆ Aligns you with the ball

◆ Allows you to transfer your weight comfortably into the stroke, giving you power and consistency

Recently, Gordon, a "B"-level, new student, came to me complaining that he had leveled off a few years ago and had not improved his game since. His goal was to become an "A" (5.0) player. He had seen various pros and had worked consistently on his strokes, but he could not seem to compete in singles with the "A" players at his club.

We began the lesson hitting, and sure enough, his strokes were sound and polished: topspin off both sides; fluid, high finishes; and a nice chip backhand. I figured that his serve must be the thing holding him back, so I had him hit a few. Nope, that wasn't it. He had good motion, reasonable speed, and a good kick second serve. So I said, "Let's play a few points."

Then it began: the mishits, over-running the ball, and a general disorientation when he hit on the run. In fact, Gordon's beautiful strokes basically turned into out-of-balance, jerky motions, over- and underhitting the moment he had to move to the ball. He couldn't properly position himself to the ball, and he didn't move his feet after he completed his stroke. He would just stand there flat-footed and wait for the ball to come to him. In addition, Gordon took large steps toward the ball, and he reacted slowly, causing him to hit awkwardly and too late.

I told Gordon that the best way to improve his overall game was to improve his footwork. He had to do court drills (with and without the racket), jump rope, run, and train his feet to move like a tennis player.

It took Gordon two weeks just to get the feel for jumping rope, and another three weeks to get himself to consistently split-step and side-step while on the court. However, after six weeks, Gordon was seeing a dramatic improvement in his technical game, as well as in his performance on the court—with respect to competition. He started to enjoy playing matches more and more. His footwork breathed fresh life into his game, and he is now a strong "A" player. He's also in much better shape, he looks and feels more like a "real player," and his strokes are holding up in the heat of battle.

Everybody wants to work on their arm motion and their style. However, not enough emphasis is placed on footwork, and that is what probably accounts for 75 percent of people's games, both good and bad. Work on your footwork, and it will make things easier on your arm, as well as on the rest of your body.

Think about how much you practice hitting the ball. If you've played for over five years, you probably hit the ball with a fairly consistent stroke. In fact, it's your position relative to the ball that dictates what your arm is forced to do. When you're too close to the ball, for example, you have to swing in a cramped and tight manner to compensate for your poor position. At that point, you will most likely "open up" (to the net) and either spray the ball long, dump it in the net, or mishit.

When you're where you want to be with relation to swinging at the ball, the actual stroke seems relatively simple and on-balance. When you're out of position at the time you should be hitting the ball, the stroke feels off-balance and cumbersome. That's why you play better when your pro feeds the balls directly to you or when you're playing against the ball machine, as opposed to when you're playing someone who makes you move or hits "junk"—that is, the use of excessive spins without much pace.

Tennis is a game of inches, so you want to be in as perfect a position as possible. This means you want to adjust and even readjust, due to misjudgments, wind, bad bounces, spin, and so on before you hit the ball.

Move On-Balance

Moving on-balance is certainly a principle of tennis that is often overlooked, but it has great value when it comes to stroke efficiency. You'll find that if you pay attention to your balance on all strokes, you'll most certainly play better tennis.

Bill, a student I had last year, came to me complaining of difficulties on the first volley; coming into net, either off the serve or on a "chip and charge" play. He said that he had no trouble once he was into net, but the transition off the first volley was completely erratic. When I asked him where the first volley would go, he said, "Everywhere." Wow. I had to see this for myself.

So, Bill played a practice set against one of my steadier students so we could see where the problem was. It only took a couple of serve-and-volley points for me to see that Bill was completely off-balance when he hit the first volley. He was either moving through the hit with his shoulders dipping forward and his rear end in the air, or he would try to stop and get low with the ball, but would end up catching himself, falling off-balance. Either way, he found, not surprisingly, that the first volley felt awkward and overly strenuous.

We discussed my observations and decided that he should try the next few points, concentrating on keeping his shoulders level, chin up, and trying to hit with his center of gravity lowered, by dropping his back knee toward the ground. The improvement was dramatic. Not only did Bill look more stable and relaxed, but he seemed to hit the ball with more confidence and authority. By centering his weight and keeping his movements coming from his waist, as opposed to leaning over the ball, he found that it was easier to move, to hit, and even to judge the ball.

Things always seem different in a warm-up than they do in a match, though. Balance is one of those concepts that will make a difference. When you're relaxed and not "pushed," it's more comfortable to hit and, therefore, easier to play well. When someone else pushes you, you get off-balance and out of the "flow."

"Move from your waist" is another rule that will help you to not only stay on-balance, but also make you faster and more powerful. Your movements should come from the center of your body, your diaphragm. You want to avoid leaning over when you run to the ball or side-step back to the center. This might feel like you're getting a "jump" on the ball, but in actuality, it slows you down because you're running "top-heavy." Therefore, it takes wasted energy just to stay on-balance. Move from the center of your body, your waist, and you'll move more gracefully and with more speed and power.

One-handers often have trouble keeping their balance because they swing their back hip, foot, and even their nonhitting hand into the hit to help them get more power out of their shot. Please don't. It doesn't necessarily give you more power; but what it does do is cause you to mishit and play inconsistently. Just line yourself up with the ball, swing, and remain sideways and on-balance. (Remember the capital "T" in the chapter on backhands.)

One sure-fire way to hold your balance on the one-handed back-hand is to throw your left hand back behind you at the same time you swing at the ball. Symmetrically, as you swing your hitting hand forward to the ball, you "split" your opposite hand straight behind you, forming a capital "T." Done correctly, this will ensure that you do not open up and fall off-balance. Additionally, keep your back foot on the ground, and don't let it pivot, as on the forehand. In fact, when Billie Jean King used to hit backhands on the run, I noticed that she would often kick her back foot behind her as she swung, keeping her sideways. Good idea. Try it.

In theory, the one-hander can be hit while sitting in a chair. There is no need to "open up," pivot the back foot, or move. It is best hit when your body is on-balance so that your hitting arm is allowed an uninterrupted flow toward the ball. Remember, unlike the forehand, your body is not in the way of your "follow-through." You can, therefore, position yourself, let your arm swing (like a door) on a hinge (your shoulder), and maintain your balance.

Volleys and pick-ups in the mid-court, as opposed to ground-strokes, should be taken generally from a lower center of gravity, bringing your torso closer to the ground. There are exceptions, however, primarily for those players who can't stay on-balance because they just cannot bend their knees properly. The following is really the best and only way to get down for a low volley:

First, split-step so that you can move explosively to the ball. Then, as you're stepping toward the low volley, gently drop your back knee to the ground. This ensures that you're moving forward to the ball, while your torso remains straight and comfortably erect as you hit it. Dropping your back leg enables you to keep your back straight, and helps you keep your body stable and on-balance. This balanced feeling can be further enhanced by keeping your shoulders level and your chin up.

The above movement takes a certain amount of practice to acquire the strength and muscle memory. Try to get someone to feed you balls while you just sit on your back knee (front foot up), and volley them back. Do this exercise until it feels comfortable. You'll like the fact that you're looking right at the ball instead of leaning on top of it.

A good drill to reinforce this movement is to get in your "ready position" (with or without your racket), split-step, move one or two steps to the right, and pretend to hit a volley, dropping your back knee to the ground while stepping forward. Then, stand up, take a side-step or two, split again, and take two steps in the other direction. Make sure that your back is straight, your chin is up, and you're in complete control and balance. Gently let yourself down on each knee, and with controlled strength, pop back up to your ready position, staying low the whole time. Continue this drill until your legs start to burn, and then do a couple more.

Until you've mastered the movements for low volleys, you should volley *comfortably*. Don't lean over the ball trying to get "low." You're much better off keeping your back fairly straight and your legs just slightly flexed, and maintaining a very comfortable and stable position. You'll see the ball better, and your arm will move more fluidly and have more control. John McEnroe used to jump when hitting half-volleys, and do it with great consistency and success.

Six Steps to Better Footwork

Learn the footwork of real players, and bring your entire game to a higher level. It's not just a matter of being fast. There is technique involved. Here are a tennis player's dance steps:

1. Bounce Step
2. Split Step
3. Sprint Step
4. Stutter Step
5. Impact Step
6. Side Step

1. Bounce Step. The bounce step keeps your feet alive and moving. The idea of the bounce step is to stay light on your feet and bounce from foot to foot while the ball is in the opponent's court. The bounce step is where everything begins: your momentum, your anticipation, and your speed to the ball.

Keeping your feet bouncing or jogging in place is like leaving your motor in idle. You can generate speed more quickly, and it takes less gas. Keep bounce-stepping when you're in between hits (that is, when you're not hitting the ball).

Here is where you turn your tennis into an aerobic sport. Additionally, the bounce step keeps you light-hearted and focused. Remember, keep your feet moving throughout the point.

2. *Split Step.* We talked about split steps in the previous section on preparation, but this step is so important to becoming an "A" player that it's worth reiterating. This is probably the single most understated and underrated lesson in the art of learning to move and play. The split step is what can get you two steps closer to every wide shot, as well as get you out of the way of those balls that tend to jam you. A proper split step can turn your game around single-handedly.

The split step, simply put, is a small jump where you land on the balls of your feet upon impact (when your opponent's racket makes contact with the ball). You jump about one to three inches off the ground, landing evenly, shoulder-width apart, with your knees comfortably bent and your hands in front of you. You want to feel the strength coming from the center of your body, your legs flexed and poised to move. Your hips should be parallel to the net, and your shoulders should be neither hunched over nor tilted back. This is a position of strength, and it is from this position that you "push off" in the direction of the ball coming off your opponent's strings.

Develop the habit of split-stepping every time your opponent hits the ball: whether you're   in the backcourt or up at net. The advantage of split-stepping with good timing is that it enables you to move (or shall I say "spring") quickly in any direction. You can virtually cover the net from the center line with one good split step.

If you've ever watched the Wimbledon championships, you might have noticed that toward the end of the tournament, the grass is mutilated at the service line, on both sides of the court. This erosive phenomenon occurs due to all the serve-and-volley players. They run to net on the way after serving, split-step, and then push off to their volley. Most pros make it to the service line when they make their split-step. If you watch them, you'll see how they've perfected their timing. In fact, this step flows so well that you might not pay attention to it. Start noticing, though, because the split step is a major reason why they get around the court so beautifully.

3. *Sprint Step.* Now that you're balanced and poised to spring (like a cat) to the ball the moment it leaves your opponent's strings, let's get there. Run! Move from your navel, the center of your body. Coming off of a good split step and being centered will make your push-off and first steps explosive. Take powerful, long strides, as if you were running a 50-yard dash. Race to the ball! Your goal for each shot is to beat the ball to the bounce on groundstrokes. Remember, move from your waist, not your shoulders.

4. *Stutter Step.* This footwork technique is used as you near the ball in order to set up for your final position before the stroke. Instead of long, powerful steps, they now become short, quick, up-and-down movements. These steps ought to produce a squeaking noise on hard courts. Should you perform the optimum footwork, which is get to the ball early (before it bounces), you'll almost be running quickly in place, waiting for the ball. This little dance step allows you to re-adjust and fine-tune your position to the ball. Remember, your steps get smaller and smaller the closer you (a) get to the ball; and (b) get to the net.

    There are two exceptions: (1) When you're hitting a ball on the dead run, and (2) when you're sprinting to put away a "floater" at net before it drops below the height of the net.

5. *Impact Step.* This is the final step you make just before (or as) you hit the ball. After you've gotten to the ball and have stutter-stepped your way to a good position, you take your final step to the hit. Step forward toward the net, or even better, toward your hitting destination if possible. Try to avoid stepping outside the court or toward either of the side fences. You want your weight distribution and "flow" going toward the ball and the court.

   Your impact step should be comfortable, about shoulder-width apart. Don't take so large of a step that you can't maintain your balance at impact. You want your step large enough, however, so that you have a strong base from which to hit. It is best to step with your foot pointed somewhat into the court; not completely sideways to the net. It is more difficult to transfer your weight comfortably, especially on forehands and two-handed backhands, where you'll need to pivot your back foot completely.

6. *Side Step.* Once you've hit the ball, get back to the center of the court by side-stepping. This running style implies that you face the net (and your opponent) while you move in a sideways fashion on the balls of your feet, clicking your heels together with each stride. Once again, you want to move from your navel, keeping your body stable and balanced, able to move in any direction forward or back, left or right, with the same degree of strength, agility, and stability. If you turn and run back to the center, your opponent will trip you up by hitting to the direction you just came from, "wrong-footing" you. Consider your stroke complete only after you've side-stepped back to your recovery position.

Move Like a Cat at Net

Stay graceful. Keep your torso straight, legs flexed, with your chin up, so you can move more quickly and with more coordination. Drop your back knee toward the court on low volleys, keeping your shoulders level and your chin up. By lowering your back knee to the ground, your eyes are on the same level as the ball, on-balance. It's easier to stay relaxed. I've noticed that when players try to get too low, bending at the waist, they look panicky and uncoordinated on their volleys. So, shoulders level, chin up—even if you don't get quite as low, you have a more relaxed and efficient view of the ball, making the stroke easier to execute.

However, if you can't get your back knee bent, keep your chest lifted and your shoulders level, as it's easier to view the strings of your racket making contact with the ball. If you lean over the ball from your waist, it gives you a cock-eyed view of the ball; you end up looking down on it, losing your depth perception and your peripheral view of the court.

An exercise to try: Lunges are a good exercise to build strength in your legs for low volleys and for helping you spring back up in the ready position.

Low volley shadow drill: Start low, hand in front, with or without a racket. Take a small hop and a skip, and slowly come to your back knee and step across as if you were volleying. Spring up and do the same thing on the other side, and continue: right knee, left knee, and so on. Increase your stamina by building up from 10 to 15 times, on up.

Position Yourself for Easy Overheads

Once you're committed to hitting the back of the ball, positioning is everything. To hit the back of the ball, you've got to *see* it. It's essential for powerful and consistent overheads. It's what makes the overhead easy. Improper positioning makes the overhead next to impossible for most club players.

So get ready for your overhead, and side-step back quickly. Get the ball slightly off to the right (or the left if you're left-handed) as you move sideways to the net. Also, get yourself in position behind the ball. Don't let it drift over your head. It's always easier to move forward at the last moment than back. Plus, when you hit the overhead, you want your weight moving forward. Also, as you see the lob coming, get your hitting hand back, either behind your head, with your racket down your back, or pointing the tip of your racket at the ball. But get your hitting hand behind your head immediately. It might be coming faster than you think. Do not let the ball get behind you!

◆   ◆   ◆

The *scissors-kick* is a flamboyant and effective *jump* that the pros and other good players use when the lob gets behind them. The problem is that it is overtaught, overused, and usually counterproductive in either club play or even "A"-level tennis. It gives many players the impression that they can lag on their overhead preparation. Get back to the overhead early, and you won't have to jump at the last moment. But if you absolutely have to, go ahead and jump.

The Serve-and-Volley Dance

"Serve-one, two, three, split-step." That's how it goes. Make your serve, get to net as fast as you can, and when your opponent makes contact, split-step. This give you a slight hesitation to decide which way to move (or not). As you get closer to the net, or to any ball for that matter, you get lower and your steps get smaller. Keep your hands in front of you, your chin up (no stooping from the waist), and make sure to "split" and push toward the ball, low and tight, the moment your opponent makes contact. Cut off any angle by always moving through the center of the court toward the ball (and toward the net). Never move backwards or directly sideways to any volley. Keep your shoulders level as you go to the ball.

Chapter Eight

FLOW WITH THE GAME:

RHYTHM, BALANCE, AND TIMING

Most of the people in the tennis world will tell you that the only way to develop the intangibles of tennis—that is, the tennis nuances such as timing and anticipation—is to play more tennis. To some degree, that's true. However, there are definitely some ways in which you can accelerate your learning curve.

Get into the Rhythm of the Game

Getting into the rhythm of the game means learning to get into the "flow" with respect to the movement of the ball, your opponent, and the game itself. By finding just the right rhythm, you'll move and hit more effortlessly and with more fluidity. A lack of rhythm, on the other hand, will prevent you from getting to the ball on time, forcing you to rush shots or hit balls with unnecessary effort. You just won't feel like you're really in the game.

I recently went to watch the finals of a tournament that two of my 4.0 (above-average) students were playing, and I saw a dramatic comeback. Tom and Dave were down 6-4, 5-3, 40-15 in the second set, returning against a server whom they hadn't broken all day, when they went into a brief five-second conference. Four returns, two volleys, and one overhead later, the score was 5-4 "on-serve," and a whole new ball game developed.. They went on to win 7-6, 6-4.

After the match, I congratulated the guys on their win, and I asked them what happened at that critical double-match point. They told me that Tom had said to Dave, "Okay, breathe through your nose and 'toss, hit, bounce, hit.' That's it! That's all we did! The returns went in cross-court and low, and we played four good points!"

What Tom and Dave did was to block out all the other noises and static that can go through your mind under pressure by breathing through the nose. Next, they created a rhythm on the return of serve by using a method that I call "toss, hit, bounce, hit." This is a technique whereby you shout commands as they happen, creating an internal rhythm in concert with the flight of the ball (which I'll explain in depth later in this chapter).

By Getting into the Rhythm of the Game, You'll:

◆ Hit with better timing
◆ Stroke with fluidity
◆ Feel like you're a part of the entire game
◆ Stay energized throughout the match
◆ Get and stay in the point
◆ Boost your self-confidence

Although this is a brief chapter, the points I'm presenting can really make a difference in your overall play. Rhythm can make or break a match for you. With it, you'll feel loose, warmed up, and natural; without it, you'll feel awkward and "out of sync." Practice the following techniques, and you'll reap the benefits of good timing and flowing strokes on the court.

Talk the Ball into Your Racket

"Back, bounce, hit!" This method helps you develop a rhythm with the ball while hitting your groundstrokes. It is a series of commands that, verbalized at the appropriate times, can help you hit with greater ease and fluidity and actually help you to see the ball better.

Here's how it works: The moment your opponent makes contact with the ball, you say to yourself, "Back." This command is your cue to react and turn your body immediately. Just as the ball bounces on your side of the court, you say, "Bounce," and at that point you plant your feet. Ideally, at this moment, all movement stops. Then, as your racket comes forward and actually makes contact with the ball, you say to yourself, "Hit."

The important thing to remember is that you say these commands just as they happen. Don't say "back" and take your racket back a second later. That defeats the whole purpose. The command must be spoken silently or aloud at the actual moment of contact. This technique helps you to accomplish two things: First, it forces you to glue your eyes to the ball from the moment it hits your opponent's racket to the time it hits yours. In addition, this method helps you move your feet, prepare early, and get into a rhythm that's in sync with your opponent's. This technique is especially useful during your pre-game warm-ups.

You'll find that every opponent you play has a definite and distinct rhythm that you'll lock into with this method. A rhythmic pattern will develop, which will help you anticipate better, move to the ball with more time to spare, and feel as if you're in control of the pace of the match. You'll develop a more centered and calm relationship with the ball. The rhythm will remain fairly constant with each person you play; therefore, you'll feel more at one with the ball and the game as a whole. Some players prefer to only say the "bounce-hit" part. Do what works.

Hit at Three-Quarter Speed

Another technique is to hit at three-quarter speed. Many players who feel fatigued or who are under pressure will resort to either over-hitting or "pushing." It's important to develop a speed that you can rely on that is consistent, accurate, and efficient—one that can get the job done. Three-quarters of your fastest speed is the optimal pace. It's fast enough to pass your opponent, and it's controllable so you can keep the ball in play.

This speed is especially useful when you're beginning a match. It helps you get into the rhythm and flow of the game, while keeping the pressure on your opponent.

Rhythm on the Return of Serve

A variation on "back, bounce, hit" is "toss, hit, bounce, hit" on the return of serve. Just as your opponent throws the ball up on the serve, you say, "Toss." As your opponent makes contact with the ball, you say, "Hit." Then when the ball lands in the serving box, you say, "Bounce." Finally, when you hit the ball, you say, "Hit!" This method helps give you the rhythm that you need to feel comfortable returning a serve. In addition, it will help you prepare early, by focusing in on, and moving to, the ball.

You should use this method every time you go to return a serve, and especially when someone has a fast or difficult-to-return serve. It will help you feel more comfortable on the court and get into the flow of the match.

Rhythm at the Net

There's a definite rhythm that's called for when it comes to playing a good net game. Why is it that some people get to net and immediately become either victims of lobs and passing shots, or virtual targets? On the other hand, why is it that other players are so good at net that their opponents can't seem to get a ball past them? Nine times out of ten, the great players at net are the ones who have good rhythm on their "split steps," which gives them good timing when moving to their volleys and overheads.

While playing net, tell yourself to "split" when your opponent hits the ball, and "step" as you go to hit the volley. "Split-step, split-step." This will help get your rhythm going with respect to your footwork at net.

Know Your Racket Face

It's really important to know what your racket face is doing! If your racket face is too open, the ball goes up, and depending on the speed of the racket when it hits the ball, you could either hit a lob, drop-shot, or simply hit it out. You could master all of the other rules, but if you can't control the face of your racket at the contact point, you'll never have any consistency in your game on a daily basis.

Not too long ago, I noticed that Rick, one of my "A" (or 5.0) students, was resorting to a chip forehand on most of his returns of serve and approach shots. It was obvious that he felt as if this was a safer return than trying to hit flat or topspin. What wasn't obvious was why it felt safer. The reason many players fall back on chips under pressure is because they feel it's easier to control the racket face if they just hold the racket flat to the ball and push it forward. This would have been fine for Rick if all he wanted to do was win the first round or two of a tournament. This type of stroke used on a consistent basis can only get you past a certain level of player. Rick was making it past the first few rounds regularly, but he couldn't beat the top players in the later rounds. I felt that a bad habit was forming, which had to be addressed before it became too ingrained.

Rick and I discussed the fact that playing it too safe against tournament-tough players will only allow you to "hang in there." Rick needed to dictate the pace and take control of the big points, which meant that he'd have to do more than just "counter-punch." If he wanted to break into an even higher level of the game, he would have to start going for more of the shots that we knew he had the capability of hitting, and stop just getting the ball in play, even off of big serves. There are more aggressive shots that can be hit with the same margin of safety as a block shot, as long as the player has a keen awareness and command over the face and head of his or her racket.

Rick spent the next hour making a point of being aware of his racket face at all times. I told him that if he needed to, he could shorten his backswing returning fast serves, but no chipping or blocking. He made sure that no matter what shot he hit, the face of his racket was always parallel to the net, never opening or closing. When it came to returning serve, I told Rick to play the next couple of sets hitting away on returns, and not to chip any returns no matter how hard the serve. If Rick was to become a top player, he would have to gain confidence in swinging under pressure, which meant he would have to have the same degree of control over his racket face as he did on the block.

Suffice it to say, Rick's biggest weapon, from that afternoon onward, became his return of serve—and it continues to get more powerful. The more he hit, the more great returns he made, and the more his confidence rose. His biggest weapon turned out to be his knowledge and command of the racket face. Rarely does he ever use the chip forehand, unless he's coming behind it up to net.

Having control over the racket face is as important for beginners trying to keep the ball in the court as it is for tournament players going for "touch" shots or "great gets."

Controlling Your Racket Face Will Help You:

- ◆ Keep the ball in play
- ◆ Control the depth and placement of your shots
- ◆ Hit with more touch (that is, lobs and drop shots)
- ◆ Make "great gets"
- ◆ Improve your overall timing
- ◆ Return "junk," power, and "no-pace" balls with ease

Having full control over your game means having control over your racket head. For most players, groundstrokes require the racket head to come through with the handle and the rest of the racket. However, serves and overheads require headweight, whereby the racket head leads the way, producing quicker head speed and, therefore, more power. Also, the serve, as we've illustrated, requires a mastery over the racket edge, which sends the racket face to the ball and produces a variety of spins.

The top players set themselves apart from the "first-rounders" by using a variety of weapons. Drop shots, lobs, angle volleys, off-pace shots, and extra-pace shots are all a part of an "A" player's arsenal. Touch is acquired by knowing the face of your racket and by pacing your shots accurately. Most beginner/intermediate players can hit the ball in the court until they try to put a little more pace on their shot. That's when they turn over their wrist or "open up the face," and then they lose the ball. Some players have trouble controlling the face when no-pace balls are hit to them and they have to generate all the pace; others lose control when the ball comes over too fast.

Hit On-Balance

As I've mentioned previously, being on-balance is essential to all strokes. I mean, think about it: What's easier—hitting a free-throw in basketball with time to set up, or hitting a fade-away jumper with some defenseman's hand in your face? Even when you watch the pros hit the ball while leaping into in the air, notice that they're in complete control. Andre Agassi, for example, jumps into the ball and uses his weight for power, as opposed to catching himself falling off-balance.

One technique for hitting your groundstrokes on-balance is to "hold your finish." You should be able to hit a forehand or backhand stroke and hold that finish for at least a count of "one-one thousand, two-one thousand" without falling off-balance. If you cannot hold your balance that long, then you need to correct that problem, and here's how to do just that:

Forehands and two-handed backhands should generally be finished with the back foot pivoted (rolling on the toe with the heel facing the sky). Usually people will fall off-balance because they try to hold this back foot down. They end up falling onto that same foot as they swing (or immediately afterwards), because their momentum of the swing carries them forward. Let the toe roll, and you'll find it easy to hold your finish comfortably. This applies to the two-handed backhand as well, because it is merely a left-handed forehand. On both strokes, in order to finish completely you must get your body out of the way of your hitting arm (open up), so that your arm can come "through." There are only three ways to do that: (1) Pull your front foot away, (2) swing your back foot around, and (3) pivot the back foot. Pivoting is the only way to "open up" without "pulling off the ball" and falling off-balance.

Next, let's dismiss the "bend your knees" theory once and for all on groundstrokes. What does that mean? Is it reality? Why do Chang, Agassi, and countless other players jump when they hit their topspin or flat groundstrokes? Bending you knees came about because 30-plus years ago tennis was played with Eastern grips, closed stances, and "flat" shots. The game was more finesse and less power. It was thought that you should swing straight through. Everyone agreed that you needed to bend your knees. Many pros even taught, "Racket straight back and straight forward. Point to the top of the net."

There are so many different styles today that you're hard-pressed to find two professional players who play exactly the same. Today's game calls for topspin as a necessity, because the game is faster, the rackets are bigger, and everyone hits harder. In fact, tennis masters hit topspin forehands off either foot. To do that, you must let the racket—not your body—go from "low to high" as it's contacting the ball.

Bending your knees can actually hinder that type of swing, and also make your stroke more uncomfortable and stiff. It's a very unathletic position, making most players feel tight and awkward. Crouch down with your racket in your hand. See how that feels. That uncomfortable feeling is certainly not conducive to a smooth stroke. It's definitely easier (and certainly more graceful), to perform your best when you're as relaxed as possible. Try hitting your groundstrokes while you stand tall, instead of crouching low and bending your knees. You can even exaggerate and stand taller than usual (even when hitting low balls). See if this makes you feel more on-balance, fluid, and adept. Also, you'll find it easier to put more topspin on the ball, because now you're letting your racket get below the ball, making it easier to rise at the point of contact and beyond.

◆ ◆ ◆

Early preparation and footwork taught you to beat the ball to the bounce, which enables you to hit on-balance. So keep in mind: Hustle. Hustle to the ball in the backcourt and up at net. Hustle back to the center in between hits. By staying ahead of the ball, you have a better chance of hitting on-balance. And in the same breath, the better your footwork is, the easier it is to get in good position early. On lobs, get back quickly; don't dawdle. If you can take the shot moving forward on-balance, don't wait and reach behind or jump at the last second. That's making an easy put-away into a great get. Many players like to incorporate the scissors-kick into their overhead. That's not a good idea. The scissors-kick should be used as a last resort on a great lob. Why make an easy shot hard? Get back early, step in, and "knock it off." That way your weight can be transferring forward at the hit. Get to groundstrokes early so you can hit with the most comfortable base below you.

Even when you're on the full run, up in the air making a high backhand volley or backing away from a ball hit right at you on the serve, try to keep a sense of balance about you so that you can swing with a degree of composure and control. Keep your eyes on the ball, and try to keep your shoulders even and stable while you make contact during these acrobatic maneuvers. Be conscious of keeping your body relaxed and in control. Don't fall down while you're hitting! Keep either your hips, feet, or upper body stable, and always keep looking at the hit— even past the hit. It's best, of course, to keep your entire body under control.

Even when you see the pros leave their feet, such as Sampras on his serve and Becker on his diving volleys, they do it with control. They're using their weight to generate more power and not just to stay on-balance. Jumping into a topspin forehand is much different from falling away from one. Remember, even when you're hitting cross-court, you still lean toward the ball and not toward the court you're hitting to. You can't pull the ball to where you want it to go. Concentrate on the ball, and angle the face more to the area you're hitting to.

◆ ◆ ◆

Rhythm, balance, and control of your racket face, along with maintaining your focus on the ball, are what will help you develop good timing. If you feel like you're losing your timing, get it back by either doing the "back, bounce, hit" exercise; by "seeing the spot"; or by "freezing your finish." Whatever you do, stay calm enough to think. Once you lose your cool, you'll "space out," and you won't be able to think yourself back into the game.

Chapter Nine

◆ ◆ ◆ ◆ ◆

THE NECESSARY SPECIALTY SHOTS

Trick shots, or specialty shots, have always been a solid foundation for my own game (coming from a clay court background). I can't tell you how many matches I've won with drop shots, stop volleys, and lobs. You've got to have these shots if you want to call yourself a player. Try some of the following techniques for mastering tennis specialty shots. You'll find them useful.

Keep in mind that for these shots, racket-face control is key. The better your control, the better your "touch" (or "feel") on all your shots, particularly these specialties. Having racket-face control can also help you when you're out of position or in trouble, but you still need to make your shot go to a particular spot on the court.

Drop Shots Are Fun

The drop shot is a more intricate stroke than the forehand and backhand, because this shot requires that you adjust the edge of your racket face during the shot. You have to be a master of the face and racket-head speed in order to hit a consistently good drop shot.

Some people think that the drop shot is just a lightly hit ball. Others think it is a short jab (half-stroke) at the ball. But, in fact, you might find that you take a longer stroke than you do on your groundstrokes. You need "length" to stay "on the ball" longer, giving you greater control. So, elongate the stroke. Additionally, you'll see now how the drop shots are stroked differently from the groundstrokes.

Warning: The drop shot is almost impossible to hit correctly with a Western grip. You'll need to switch to either a continental or Eastern grip, one where your "face" is open to, or at least perpendicular to, the net.

Remember that your drop shot is only as good as its disguise. You want your opponent to think that you're about to crack that short ball hard and deep for a winner or approach shot. Set your opponent up so he or she doesn't think it's coming. If you look like you're hitting a drop shot (in a blocking position, rather than a stroking one), then it will be easy to read. Even the best-hit drop shots can then be tracked down. I've found that for most players the most effective drop shots (and the easiest to master), are hit within five feet of the service line and at about shoulder height.

Disguise the drop shot, approaching the ball as if you're going to drive it hard and deep.

So, what you need to do is step up to the ball, pretend to take your full groundstroke swing, but as you get within inches of the ball, you back off—that is, slow your swing down quickly, yet smoothly, as if your racket just ran into a pool of water. Keep it smooth. No jerking motions, and don't stop at the contact point.

Now, just as you slow your racket down to hit the ball, begin to open the face gradually until it's making contact with the underside of the ball, with your racket parallel to the court. Roll your racket face along the bottom of the ball to give the ball "backspin," which makes the ball "die" once it hits your opponent's court.

Open your racket face, strings facing up to the sky. This brushes (or rolls) the bottom of the ball, causing "backspin."

Continue the stroke by leading out toward the net with the bottom edge of the racket head. Finish with your racket high and the racket face "open." This will continue to increase the backspin on the ball. It's a real "feel" or "touch" shot, and takes an enormous amount of control over the racket head.

On both forehand and backhand drop shots, finish high, bringing the bottom edge of the racket up. A slow, long stroke, it takes time to develop a soft hand, racket-face control, and timing.

The drop shot is one of tennis's foremost finesse shots. I think if you're a 5.0 (or above) player, or a junior tournament player, you should be able to make a majority of your drop shots. It's a phenomenal shot to have in your arsenal, as it opens up several more strategies. An effective drop shot hit at the appropriate time can outsmart your opponent. Use it every so often to mix the game up, especially on big points. It also comes in handy when you're having trouble battling groundstrokes with your opponent. Also, very often you play someone who is short, slow, doesn't move "up and back" quickly, or is just out of shape. The drop shot gives you another weapon to use against this type of player.

Drop Shot Practice:

1. A good drill for racket-face control and touch is a game called *dinkum.* It's played with you and a practice partner. The boundaries are the singles lines from the net to the service lines. Start with both of you standing at the center strap, opposite one another at net. One player drops the ball on top of the net so that the ball falls on the opponent's side. That starts the point. The only rule is that you cannot hit the ball in the air (volley); the ball must bounce. You can use angles, drop shots, and even lobs, so long as they stay inside the service line. No hard or downward-sloped shots. This drill will not only help you with your mastery over the racket face and the speed of the head, but it will help you immensely with your footwork, agility, speed, and endurance.

2. Set the ball machine so it hits to the service line, a little high and slow, and practice drop-shotting. Once you're hitting the ball well from there, go farther back in the court.

3. With a basket of balls at your side, drop the ball between the service line and the net, and hit your drop shots. Try to hit enough underspin so that after the ball bounces, it comes back

toward the net. When you get real control and "feel," you can try to make the ball hit just to the other side of the net, and bounce back over the net to your side.

Two visuals for a better drop shot:

1. Having trouble rolling the bottom of the ball? Try to push the racket head through as if you were shoving a pizza in the oven.

2. Having trouble "backing off" on the swing? Pretend you're swinging into a pool of water, and just as the racket hits the ball, it slows down.

On the Drop Shot, Remember to:

 ◆ Disguise

 ◆ "Back off"

 ◆ Open the face

 ◆ Elongate the stroke; keep it smooth

The "Stop" (Drop) Volley

This shot is used quite a bit at the pro level, but not nearly enough at the club or intermediate levels. It's a great off-pace shot that can not only help you win a point when your opponent is deep in the backcourt, but which also provides a psychological weapon, keeping your opponent guessing. This shot, for most players, is easier and more effective off the forehand volley. McEnroe had the most consistently lethal stop volley. I mean, that ball would hit and just die! That's how I formulated the method for this particular shot. It's one of those shots that looks a lot more difficult than it really is.

To effectively master the stop volley, lay your racket head back and turn your shoulders, as if you were about to hit a deep volley. Bring your racket out to the ball, and just as you're about to make contact, pull the racket head back by laying back your fingers, and thus, your wrist. The pace of the ball is absorbed by this motion. Make sure, however, that the racket face is still open to the court as you pull the head back.

The Deadly Lob

Here's another shot that requires racket-face control and "touch." Unlike the drop shot, you need not change the angle of the face (bottom edge up) during the stroke. The angle of the face stays constant.

The lob is, however, similar to the drop shot in that the racket face opens, and the more effective shots are the ones that are best disguised. The angle of the face is not nearly as open as with the drop shot. Similar to the drop shot, you want to maintain a long stroke.

You want your lob to go deep in the court, within four feet of the baseline. Therefore, you want to hit a bigger piece of the ball. And, you don't want any backspin on the ball; if anything, you'd like to eventually master the topspin lob. (I won't be teaching the topspin lob in this book, because it's merely an extreme looping topspin forehand, and I can't teach "feel." That shot is pure touch.)

The finish on the lob is high and open. Keep the wrist firm throughout the hit, keeping control of the angle of the face and the racket-head speed. The key to controlling the racket head on the lob is bringing the racket head up even with the handle. There should be very little, if any, headweight on this shot. The head banging the ball would probably cause it to go long. So, don't use any wrist.

Swing slow and even. Elongate the stroke and try to "feel" the baseline. Don't speed up or slow down at the hit, and finish high, as if you were *reaching* for your target with the palm of your hand. Remember, in singles you probably want to hit this shot to the backhand; it makes for a much tougher overhead.

Make Great Gets

In all too many cases, a match is won by one or two points. That's why it's important to try to make great gets—that is, to try to virtually rob your opponent of winners. Whether you're hitting a passing shot on the run or a backhand stab volley as the ball is going by you at net, it requires steady control of your wrist and your racket face. You have to stabilize the racket face throughout the shot, which can take some strength and discipline.

When you're diving for a wide volley that's flying past you on either side, make sure to hold the face of the racket still (by holding your wrist firm) until you actually see the strings contact the ball. Don't just flick the head of your racket (with your wrist) at the ball. Generally that will cause you to mishit or miss the ball completely.

The same thing applies to high backhand volleys where you're facing the side (and sometimes, the back fence). See the face of the racket make contact with the ball with the proper angle into the court. Don't swat down. Spend time up there until the ball has bounced off the strings and is headed into the court. Hold the racket steady so the ball can carom off of it like it would a wall.

Half-Volleys (Pick-Ups)

Pick-ups give players trouble, primarily because they turn their wrist and face over during the hit. Whether you're standing straight up or are bending down low, what matters is that your racket face is waiting in the right place and stays constant throughout the swing.

Topspin is probably the safest and most effective shot, so long as you lift the racket head up the back of the ball with the face at roughly the same angle throughout the stroke. Once again, hold the racket face steady as you see the hit. Don't use much of a backswing, use a big lift, keep your racket face flat, and keep your eyes down (on the ball).

I thought that John McEnroe had the best pick-ups in the game. He actually jumped up off the ground when he hit them. He had confidence, control, depth, and topspin. He got a little curve on the ball by reaching his head (or the tip of his racket) around the outside of the ball without breaking his wrist. This seemed to make the shot even safer. You might want to try that; come up and around the outside of the ball with the edge. Reminder: Don't turn over the head at impact; lift the edge (of the racket) straight up.

Develop a Weapon

Most club players are so worried about the weaknesses in their game that they forget to recognize and realize their strengths. It is vital that you develop one or more weapons in your arsenal that you can rely on. It doesn't really matter what it is—cross-court forehand, great volley or touch, so long as you have complete confidence. Then, when you've mastered these shots, you can call on them when you're in a pinch.

These weapons, or confidence-builders, can really change the outcome of a match. Jim Courier has the "inside-out" forehand down the line, Sampras has the serve, Chang's got the speed, and Agassi has the deadly service return. You generally find that all great players have a weapon or more. Find yours, and then practice it until you own it!

Short, low backswing, racket head perpendicular to the court.   *Lift racket head up, always staying on edge. Eyes stay down on contact.*

Chapter Ten

◆　◆　◆　◆　◆

MATCH PLAY:

DOING YOUR BEST UNDER PRESSURE

There are countless reasons why you might not be playing your best during a match. Mental and emotional static may cause you to miss easy shots, double-fault at crucial times, and generally assist you in "beating yourself." Let's look at some of those pressures and distractions:

What Pressures and Distractions Could Affect
Your Play Adversely?

◆ You're afraid to lose, to be called a loser or a failure.

◆ You're worried about what your parents or friends will think. Will they be proud of you?

◆ You're concerned about making a particular team or league.

◆ You want to improve your ranking.

◆ You're distracted by onlookers, perhaps the friends or relatives of your opponent.

◆ You're afraid of being humiliated in front of a crowd.

◆ You're playing against a "bad sport" or a cheater.

◆ You're as afraid of success as you are of failure, because winning could create unrealistic expectations—the pressure to win every time you go out there.

All of these pressures might seem (and often are) very real; however, you need to leave them behind when you step on the court (easier said than done, you're probably saying). Your focus needs to be intense; it needs to be on the ball and in the court. Here are some tried and true techniques for staying focused once you're involved in a match.

Anti-Choking Devices

Each of these techniques will get and keep your head in the match, and off other pressures or distractions. Try them all. Find one or more that work for you, and then remember to use them when you feel yourself slipping. They are all "good habits" that you should make your own, to help keep your head and your game together.

1. *Stay light on your feet.* This means moving your feet constantly, bouncing gently from side to side. These are not major impact moves; they are subtle energy-savers that place you in the action mode, in the "bounce step." Most people lull themselves to sleep by standing flat-footed and looking generally lethargic. This even happens on big points; players just freeze. The next time you watch the pros play, notice how they're always moving their feet up and down. This constant motion keeps them light on their feet and also gives them a degree of momentum toward the next shot. More important, this type of movement helps to tune up their concentration; to get their minds in gear. If you try this technique, you'll find that you'll feel more emotionally and physically stimulated, and you'll

react more quickly to the ball. Moving your feet should be part of your tennis way of life. Real tennis is an aerobic sport!

Move your feet at other times (other than during match play), too. For example, when you're drilling, always move in between hits—that is, when you're practicing cross-court forehands with your partner, bounce from foot to foot after you've hit the ball and it's crossing the net. Keep moving while you're standing in line waiting for your turn to drill. Run to pick up the balls. When you're playing practice matches, always move in between hits during a rally. Move your feet when waiting for return of serve. When you have a sitter forehand or backhand, don't just glide to it with one or two giant steps. Move your feet rapidly up and down, adjusting slightly while the ball is on its way to the bounce, and don't stop until the ball has hit the ground. Move! It helps you stay in the zone!

2. *Breathe.* Listen to your breath as it moves in and out. Remember the pre-game yoga. Just focus on your random breathing pattern, but don't force it. Or, try inhaling as the ball comes toward you, and exhaling (or grunting) as you hit the ball. Keep the air moving. Ilie Nastase used to say "whoosh" to himself throughout the stroke, to keep it smooth and fluid. Grunting at the contact is a good way to keep breathing and to keep yourself emotionally pumped up.

3. *Don't death-grip your racket.* Hold the racket loosely until it hits the ball, and squeeze the grip firmly only at the point of contact. You never need to "hammer"-grip the racket. Your body will tell you how firmly to grip the racket handle as you hit the ball. Not death-gripping the racket helps you "feel" the contact point.

4. *See the hit, and feel the court.* Look for the "spot." See the ball hit your strings. All experienced tennis players (as well as golfers and billiards players) know that you have to keep your eye on the ball, especially during contact. People often have a

tendency to pull their head away from the ball (and look at the court) just before contact. Unfortunately, that habit will not result in high-performance tennis.

Placement, depth, and power all happen on *your* side of the net, precisely at the moment that you're making contact with the ball. Your eyes should look down on groundstrokes, up on serves and overheads, and slightly to the side on volleys. In other words, become entranced by the ball, especially at the moment of impact. Look for a trail of dust leaving the ball on serves. Turn your head to see the volley. Do whatever it takes to make sure you don't look away before or during the moment of contact. Remember, the *ball is always your target.*

5. *Freeze your finish!* The only time you should stop moving your feet is during the hit, and at that time, you should hold your finish for a count of two. What this does is make you fully conscious of your follow-through and your balance. If you ever watch Stefan Edberg play, you'll see that very often when he hits a passing shot he looks like he's holding a pose for the photographers. He does this to hold his weight down on the ball and to hit on-balance. In addition, he can't help but pay more attention to the point of contact. So, freezing your finish helps you watch the ball better and hit more on-balance. On groundstrokes, you can combine this technique with touching your chin to your shoulder as you bring your racket up.

6. *Hit at three-quarter speed.* You want to find a comfortable pace at which to hit the ball, a natural swing, if you will. Don't overhit or push the ball. Try to find that one speed in between that feels loose and solid, and which also feels like it's under control. That is probably the optimal speed at which to hit for your best tennis. Everyone has a speed that is unique to him or her. Find your own and use it.

Most players think that harder is better because that's what they see the pros do on TV. Juniors and "A" or "B" players are the ones who are most prone to overhitting. The fact that the pros hit hard is possibly misleading, for they may really only be hitting at *their* three-quarter speed which, to us, looks like full speed. In addition, as a result of being on the court so frequently, their timing has developed to such an extent that they are able to hit with much greater strength.

So, practice hitting at three-quarter speed because that is the pace you'll feel the most comfortable using in a match. I see many junior tournament and competitive club players hitting incredibly hard in practice, only to slow down to half that speed in a match because they're not confident with that pace under pressure. Their hard shots are not working, so they resort to "pushing" the ball. Overhitting and underhitting are two common reasons why players lose concentration, confidence, and...*matches.*

7. *Stay low.* Try to stay as low as possible when waiting to return serve, and the closer you get to net. This helps to elevate your level of concentration by placing you in "another world," where things seem more vivid and much bigger (I'm sure you've heard players say that the tennis ball looked as big as a basketball on a particularly good day). By staying low, you have a more direct view of the ball because you're looking *at* it instead of *over* it. Time and time again, I've used this method while playing junior, college, and pro matches, and it has helped bring me into the zone, which has resulted in a number of victories.

8. *Loosen up.* Rest the racket on your nonhitting arm, hand, or fingers while you hold it loosely in your hitting hand, as you await your opponent's service wind-up. Keep bouncing gently from side to side!

9. *Visualize points.* See the result of the point you're about to play before it begins. Imagine the shot you're going to hit, which also serves a strategic function as well. Don't underestimate the

positive (and negative) effects your powerful mind is capable of in any situation.

10. *Get into ball "oneness."* Become "one" with the ball. Imagine that it holds a hypnotic attraction for you. Become fully focused upon it. "See" a string that pulls the ball into your "sweet spot" before you send it away—that is, hit the ball as if it's one of those paddle toys with the rubber ball and the elastic. Instead of just trying to hit a "dot" with a mallet, "pull" the ball into your strings and then "send" it away (as if it's on a string that goes from your opponent's racket to yours). Don't just play the ball when it's on your side.

Now, I'd like you to think about the following questions as they pertain to your match play. Could you use help in any of these areas?

1. Are you tight during the warm-up?
2. Does it take you three games or more to get "into it"?
3. Do you often lose the first set of a match?
4. Are you worried about double-faulting at critical times?
5. Do you let your opponent back in the match? Do you lose momentum?

If so, then you could benefit from the list on the next page, which comprises additional techniques that I've picked up from various coaches, playing pros, and students throughout 20 years of tournament tennis. I've categorized them in terms of specific situations where they might be most useful.

Quick Hints for Staying Focused

During the First Three Games of a Match:

◆ Get a rhythm first.

◆ Hit at three-quarter speed, then build up!

◆ Go for high-percentage shots.

◆ Force your opponent to play long points.

◆ Get a high percentage of first serves in.

◆ Go for depth more than power.

◆ Bring your passing shots "in." (Maybe your opponent's volley is weak.)

◆ Test out your lob.

◆ Return serves down the middle. Make your opponent *play.*

Throughout the Match:

◆ Move your feet.

◆ Replace a negative thought with a positive affirmation.

◆ Stay in the court as much as possible. Cut off the angles.

◆ Keep your first-serve percentage up.

◆ Evaluate your opponent's game, and how you can exploit his or her weaknesses.

◆ Get your service returns in.

◆ Keep the ball out of the net.

Playing the Big Points:

◆ Remember that the pressure is always on your opponent!

◆ Get to the net (put pressure on your opponent to make a shot).

◆ Exploit your opponent's weaknesses.

◆ Visualize before the point begins. Serve and return.

◆ When in doubt, hit down the middle and return an angle with the same angle.

◆ Return of serve: keep the racket on edge. Move forward. The stroke is primarily the middle through the finish.

◆ Move your feet vigorously.

◆ Get your first serve in!

Two More Golden Rules:

1. Play one point at a time, *and...*

2. ALWAYS look like the winner!

Now, let's pull all of this together. You might not be able to apply all of the techniques that I've presented thus far every time you play, but you'll be surprised to find that even a couple of them can turn your tennis day around. For example, if John (the tense doctor in Chapter Two), had tuned into his foot movement and listened to his breathing, there is no way that the cares of the day could have spoiled his game. Or, had he arrived at the court ten minutes early to stretch and relax, he could have gotten off to a much better and more enjoyable start. The techniques that I've offered you here will relax you, help you concentrate on your game, and allow you to play with enthusiasm and confidence. The keys to eliminating distractions are simple and in *your* hands.

I remember being asked to call the lines at a men's "A" final match a couple of years ago at a popular club in Southern California. It turned out that the club champion, who was 45 years old, was playing his nephew, a kid from UCLA who was all of 21. The older man had the edge in both skill and experience, but the match turned out to be a rout. The young man kept the ball in play and seemed to be right there, wherever the ball was. He had an answer for every shot, his returns were solid, his serves were sharp, and his footwork was effective. After a tough two-hour match, the young man disposed of his worthy opponent 6-2, 6-1, in a match that could have been a struggle all the way. The young man played his best, while his uncle played below average. Later that day, we were all enjoying the post-tournament festivities, and I had a chance to chat with the 45-year-old gentleman who had been heavily favored in the match. He said that the crowd might have bothered him a little, but that his nephew was "on," and he cashed in on his being a little "off."

I found out, after we had sat around and talked for a while, that the evening before, the uncle's baby daughter had the chicken pox, so he was in and out of bed worrying all night. He also told us that he was up for a huge job promotion and couldn't stop thinking about that during the match.

On the other hand, when the man's nephew shared his thoughts on the match, he said he hadn't even noticed that a nice crowd had assembled to watch. Clearly, he was more in the "here and now" of the match than his uncle was. He was focused. He was "in the zone." He couldn't be distracted. He enjoyed the match and went home feeling exhilarated and excited. His uncle, on the other hand, left feeling extremely dissatisfied and fatigued.

Playing in the zone doesn't come easily or naturally to most of us. It is a skill that is difficult to acquire and even tougher to maintain, especially on a day-to-day basis. Your concentration can be diluted by crowds, close calls, nerves, stress, or any number of distractions and variables. How is it that you can be up 6-2 and 30-love, and still go on to lose the second set 6-4, and the third set, 6-1? Quite simply, the majority of the time it's due to your concentration or lack thereof. You lose your edge and your focus, and consequently, the momentum shifts, and you let your opponent back into the match.

Don't Underplay; Don't Overplay

There are two habits you must acquire if you're going to be competitive. The first is, don't underplay balls that are hit easy, or hit right to you. They can be deceptively dangerous and can prove to be costly. Keep your feet moving, getting into position on balls that come to you, *especially those without much pace*. Those often become the ones that you take for granted and can sometimes cost you the game, set, or match.

In addition, don't overhit these same shots. I can't tell you how many times I've seen players set up a point perfectly, only to blow the volley because they tried to do too much. Stay calm as you approach the put-away. Just volley the ball into the open court if your opponent is out of position. You don't have to hit the line. Make the shot. Play within yourself!

Chapter Eleven

MATCH PLAY:
CREATING A GAME PLAN

Once you know how to hit the ball with some degree of proficiency and you have a "feel" for the game, it's time to come up with a system for success. Your goal is to learn how to think on the court, how to capitalize on your opponent's weaknesses, and how to take advantage of your strongest weapons. And finally, you need to learn how to win.

A few years ago, I went to watch one of my students, Phyllis, play in the finals of the women's "B"-division finals at her club. She played Wendy, a woman of approximately equal ability, with a weaker backhand but a stronger forehand. Their net games were both decent, but since neither of them came up to net much, it was basically a moot issue.

Capitalizing on Wendy's weakness, Phyllis sent four serves to Wendy's backhand, two of which she missed. The other two, Wendy returned to win those points. Phyllis won that game, but things changed from there on out. Phyllis kept hitting to Wendy's backhand, but the balls kept coming back slow and short. In fact, they were so short that they acted somewhat like an angled drop shot. Phyllis kept flying into net off-balance and either missed the shot or got passed or lobbed on the next shot.

Phyllis actually gave her opponent practice by hitting nonauthoritative shots to Wendy's backhand, making it stronger as the match progressed. The better Wendy's forehand got, the more confident she became, with Phyllis just getting more and more frustrated. By the middle of the second set, Phyllis was virtually finished. She didn't know what to do now that her opponent's weakness couldn't be exploited. Wendy had gained confidence in her weakest shot and went on to win the match in straight sets.

Phyllis's strategy, although it seemed like the logical one, backfired, leaving her with what she thought was no alternate plan of action. However, she never tried to serve and volley, and she never came in off of her opponent's second serve or weaker-hit balls. Basically, Phyllis did not assess the situation as the match went on, she didn't regroup, and she failed to brainstorm a new and more effective plan of attack. She merely stayed with a losing game. So, say it loud and say it proud: *Never change a winning game. Always change a losing game!*

Analyze Your Opponents

The key to changing a losing game is to be aware and to *be conscious*! Don't just swing the racket, and don't just focus on your own game. Your opponent has weaknesses, and he or she is probably just as nervous and self-conscious as you are. Figure out what your opponent's got and what you have to do to match up effectively—and the quicker you figure that out, the better. Keep your wits about you, and assess the situation at hand by keeping mental notes. As a matter of fact, it's a good idea to keep a notepad in your bag to write it all down. You can consider it your "player evaluation notebook." If you intend to play a lot of tournaments, your written evaluation will be an invaluable tool. You're bound to see the same (or same type of) player in another tournament, and usually sooner than you think.

Size Up Your Opponents During the Warm-Up

The first thing you'll want to do is size up your opponents during the warm-up as much as you can. Hit groundstrokes to both the forehand and backhand sides. See if your opponents' stroke production is sound. Do they miss more on one side than the other? Hit balls that bounce high and some that bounce low. Be aware of how the different shots are handled. Very often, a player hits a well-paced ball back with confidence and authority, but can't handle the "no-pace" ball. Or maybe it's the opposite. Maybe they swing late on hard-hit balls and have more confidence on the weak, short shots. Make sure to hit some balls deep and some short. Do your opponents back up on the deep balls, giving you an opportunity to come in, or at least allowing you to push them around the court? How do they move to short balls? Do they take the ball on the rise, or do they let it drop to their shoelaces (very risky!)? Do they run "off the court" for wide balls, or do they cut off the angles? Is your opponent a lefty? Take note of all these things!

Also, do your opponents have a variety of serves? Do they hit serves to the corners, or do most go to the center or to one particular spot? Do they follow the serve into net naturally, or do they step forward or toss into the court? Are they actually practicing their serve-and-volleys? Do they practice their "returns"? *You* definitely should. You want to get a sneak preview of how you're going to handle your opponents' serves (their pace, spin, and bounce).

And further, do your opponents hit any transition shots? Do they practice their approach shots a couple of times on each side? Did you see them hit very low volleys or pick-ups?

Do your opponents even have volleys? Make sure that you're not only concentrating on hitting good balls for them to volley. Observe what they do with the volley and how in control they look. Do they have racket-face control? Do they consistently volley the ball back to you? How do they move up there? Do they split-step? (If not, they probably don't move too well for great "gets.") Do they quickly and on-balance get away from balls that are hit directly at them, or do they get jammed? How do they handle high volleys? Are their volleys warmed up?

Really evaluate your opponents' weaknesses! What else can you try to discern? Have you given them enough of a variety of shots? Have you tested their speed? If you've tried to pass them at net, have you tried hitting right to them? (You might not have to pass them.) Have you run them wide? How's their lateral movement? Do they move well up and back to the ball? Have you tried a drop shot? Do they have patience to last in a long rally? (You may only have to get the ball back a few times each point.) Can they handle heavy spin, or are they intimidated by power? What grips are they using and, consequently, are high or low balls going to bother them more?

Do they seem emotional on the court? How's their demeanor out there? Do they look and act like winners? Are they showing any signs of anger or frustration? How's their focus, attention, and maturity? Do they intimidate you, or do they seem to *be* intimidated?

You want to understand as much as you can about your opponents (and get better and better at it). So often, players will fold if you get off to a quick, strong start. Let them start off on the defensive. Dictate the pace from the first point, and let them try to figure out your game.

Can you just play your game, or are you going to have to make some adjustments? Many of the same things that you looked for in the warm-up, you can continue to monitor throughout the match.

Match Analysis

While you're playing, note what type of game your opponents are playing: aggressive or defensive. Are your opponents capable of making solid shots? Are they "counter-punchers," only playing off of your power? Do they serve and volley, "chip and charge," "push," or play a more finesse ("touch") game? Are they handling your serve? What's their strategy?

How about *you?* Are you in the "flow" of the game? Do you know why you're winning? Or losing? Have you tried all of your serves, all the angles, all the spins and speeds? Do you seem to win a greater percentage of points serving and volleying or staying back on the serve? If you're losing staying back, have you tried coming in? Or vice versa? Have your opponents been to net? How have their overheads been? Check it out. Are they quick to the drop shots and angles?

If you're losing or struggling, make sure that you've tried as many shots and strategies as you're capable of to expose any and all of your opponents' weaknesses. Be confident that you've seen them hit as many different balls as you can.

If they're putting away balls, is it because you're hitting short? Which balls are they hitting consistently that seem to give *you* the most problems and give *them* the most control? Is it a high forehand down-the-line or a short, low forehand cross-court?

Be Sure to Look for:

1. Their favorite shots
2. Their biggest nemesis
3. The highest percentage of points won and lost, the way they came about, and the shots that were hit

Evaluate and Strategize

Don't let one passing shot or one lost point discourage you. Try it again. Maybe they got lucky. Serve and volley at big points as well as routine points to make sure they can handle the pressure. Some people play great until the big points and big games. See if that's who you're dealing with. Test them. Once you've sized up your opponents, you can intelligently formulate your strategy. All players have patterns. It's your job to find them and deal with them.

Player Analysis

(The following will help you form a blueprint of your opponent's game. The sooner in the match you can analyze his or her game, the quicker and more effectively you can devise a successful game plan. That is, the sooner you find the key, the sooner you can unlock the door.)

Strengths and weaknesses:
Biggest weakness:
Secondary weakness:

Strongest shot:
Second strongest:

Mobility
Up and back:
Lateral:
All-Out Speed:
Active/Passive Footwork:

Grips/strokes
Flat, slice, or topspin?
Groundies? Eastern, Western, continental grip?

Backcourt game
Down the middle?
Go for the lines?
Speed?
Depth?
Control?
Cross-court only?
Do they vary the speed, depth, and placement?

Reaction to net rusher
Lob?
Pass?
Choke?
Go wide?
Cross-court or down-the-line?

Transition game
Drop shots?
Angles?

Approach shots?
Pick-ups?
Movement?

Serve and net game
Serve-and-volley?
Strong second serve?
Hit backhand?
Down the middle?
Wide?
Flat
Topspin?
Slice?

Put volleys away
Down the middle?
Depth?
Speed?
Accuracy?

Anything else worth mentioning
Righty or lefty?
A thinker?
A whiner?
A fighter?
Patient?
Well-conditioned?

Two Types of Players to Watch Out for

1. *Steady Eddy—the Human Backboard.* Probably the most underrated strategy of all is staying in the backcourt and keeping the ball in play, especially in the early stages of a match. So many players are concerned with overpowering their oppo-

nents or moving them around that they ignore the obvious: get the ball in the court.

Jim, a student of mine, is about 5'10" and exceptionally thin. He doesn't have a particular weapon except for the fact that he can get to every ball and he never misses. Jim gets the ball back in the center of the court with medium topspin at a medium-to-slow pace (approximately 25 m.p.h.), and he has the patience to wait for his opponent to make a move. If his opponent comes in, Jim lobs over his head and sometimes passes him. Jim's greatest strength is his patience, and he can beat a lot of players.

A player such as Jim brings out the worst in most players, because they "lose" the match and their composure. He makes you beat yourself with unforced errors and built-up frustration, causing you to become increasingly dejected due to your lack of relaxation and concentration and your diminishing confidence level.

Make sure you don't become complacent out there on the court, because Jim will lull you to sleep with that "push" game. Keep your feet moving, and plan to be out there for the day. Maintain your patience; you're going to need it. Next, you'll want to see if you can wait patiently for your "short ball" opportunity, when you can come into net. Hit for the corners or sidelines, and hit with good pace. Come in and be mentally ready for a lob or series thereof.

You also might want to try bringing someone like Jim into net. Usually players of his ilk don't have "put-aways" up there. Also, see how his up-and-back movements are, instead of just his lateral ones. Turn the tables on him, so to speak.

2. *Chip-and-Charge Charlie:* These players come in on everything: their serve, your serve, behind lobs. Usually these are bigger men who want to take the net and dominate the pace. It can also mean (and more often, it does) that this player doesn't have much of a backcourt game, and he knows it. So, he comes in at every opportunity, be it a good or not-so-good time.

Trying to hit the ball hard past this guy is like throwing gas on a fire. That's his game, and presumably he knows what he's doing. Keep this player back with as many deep shots as possible. Make him come in off of a poor approach. Throw up high lobs. What this player wants is a quick-paced, hard-hitting game. Don't give it to him. Make him wait. Take your time on the court and in between points and games.

Sometimes, if you're proficient at chipping and charging, it's best to fight fire with fire, taking the net first. I find that if you take the net away from a net rusher, you confuse him by taking him out of his element.

Your job is to keep him off the net. You can do that by either keeping everything deep, or by taking the net first.

One way to keep him off the net is to get your first serves in, deep. Don't let him take a short serve and follow it in behind a block or chip. You also want to hit for the wide corners, forcing him to the sidelines and out away from the net. When you serve down the middle or right at him, you'll want to follow it in as much as possible. Slice serves are generally more difficult to come in on because they don't bounce high enough to hit a good block or chip return.

Returning serve, you'll want to try hitting a variety of shots to expose his weakest first volley. First, return down the center—get it back (at all costs). Speed and spin are not important here. See if this guy can volley a ball hit right at him. Some players volley best when they're pulled wide, but they can't do anything when the ball comes right to them. If you see that he can hit this shot, try a barrage of returns: chips, topspins, floaters, drives, angles, even lobs.

Keep him back by hitting deep. A big, looping topspin can also help keep him back. Make sure that your shots land within two to four feet of the baseline. Try moving this player from side to side, keeping him moving laterally instead of toward the net.

More Common Player-Types:
Their Games and How to Combat Them

1. *The Moonballers,* also affectionately known as *retrievers, pushers, scrappers, scramblers, human backboard*s, or *pains in the rear.*

The Game	Strategies
• Get everything back	• Get them to net—drop shot
• Generally hit with no pace	• Don't give them pace to work with
• Block ball back	• Be patient; wait for an opportunity
• Stay in the backcourt	• Don't overhit—use the lob
• Play/win long points	• Serve-and-volley, but only if it's a weapon

2. *Net-Rushers,* also commonly known as *serve-and-volleyers, chip-and-chargers, attack players* or *aggressive maniacs.*

The Game	Strategies
• Serve-and-volley	• Take the serve on the rise
• Chip-and-charge	• Take the net away—serve and volley
• Come in on anything hit short	• Hit deep—keep them off the net
• Come in behind your serve	• Try angles; get them off the court
• Usually get close to the net	• Lob (and sometimes sneak into net)

3. *Baseline Bombers,* also known as *big-hitters, backcourt players, hard-hitters,* or those who *powder, bash, smack, crush* or *blister* the ball.

The Game	**Strategies**
• Hit winners from the baseline	• Try not to give them pace
• Serve and stay back	• Drop shot—bring them into net
• Generally one side is stronger	• Hit angles; get them to hit on the run
• Solid groundstrokes— at least one weapon	• Serve-and-volley (if it's a weapon)
• Hit big returns and stay back	• Keep it away from their weapon

4. *Junk Ballers,* also known as...*junk ballers.*

The Game	**Strategies**
• Hit different spins	• Have patience
• Drop-shot/lob	• Keep moving
• Generally play the backcourt	• Watch the ball extra carefully
• Hit big spin serves	• Take the net

5. *All-Court Players.* All-court players do it all: serve, volley, have a sound backcourt game. You need to try to see what game works against these particular players. Expose their weaknesses if you can. These are "players," and they're the toughest to beat...and the most fun to play.

6. *Combination "All-Court" Players.* These are players who combine two or more of the above styles. Once again, find their weaknesses if you can, and capitalize on them. Look for patterns in their game. They usually have several, but they're difficult to locate.

Formulating a Game Plan

The following are some effective game plans that have been, and still are, used by club players and pros alike. Perhaps you'll find a couple that you could adapt to your game.

When to Serve and Volley:

Work on your serve-and-volley game in practice, because very often you're going to need it in a match. It can catch people off-guard, disrupting their rhythm and timing. Here are some optimal times to serve-and-volley. Keep an eye out for these opportunities to use this aggressive "take control" strategy:

1. Be on the lookout for those times when your opponents hit high or "floaty" returns (often this occurs off the backhand). Take advantage of volleys that are lifting above the height of the net, balls that you can catch close to the net. Do not let the ball get below the top of the net! Move!

2. If your opponents are steadier (or more patient) from the backcourt than you are, see if they can pass you or hit the lob. Note how they play under pressure. Don't play their game. If you're playing a pusher (and provided you're not one yourself), you'll lose if you play their game. Remember, they get more practice at this game than you do.

3. On the big points, take control. Go for shots; go to net. Drop shot...lob. Do something! Work with your adrenaline and reflexes. Put the pressure on your opponents to do something by "doing something" yourself. Take them by surprise, and go in and take the match—especially on game points and tie-break situations.

4. If your opponents continually win by chipping and charging on your serve, get in before they do. *You* take the net away from them. Don't just stay back and wait for them.

5. On good second serves, surprise them. Go into net behind them. If you're ahead, maybe hit a big second serve (and steal some momentum). Sometimes an element of surprise is just enough to throw off a player's rhythm, timing, or concentration.

6. Note when your opponents are hitting everything down the middle. Maybe they can't aim or aren't confident hitting close to the lines. Go into net and see.

7. Take control of the match's "energy" when you feel you can physically overpower or psychologically intimidate your opponents because you're bigger, taller, stronger, or smarter. Use all of your weapons. Look like the winner...always!

8. If you're losing by serving and staying back, then do something different. Always change a losing game. Maybe something else will work. Watch, listen, and think.

9. When you're tense and tight, very often you can work through your nerves by being aggressive. Even if you're still nervous, sometimes that can work for you up at net—that is, by making great gets. You can play better net (where the stroke is very short) than you can in the backcourt, where, in general, you want to remain loose and fluid.

10. In doubles—a real doubles match is played with both players up at net, whenever possible.

11. This is not a book about doubles play, but if it were, it would read: "...in doubles always be on the lookout to poach. Every point!"

Other General-Purpose Strategies: "Pro" Favorites

1. Hit deep and down the middle until your opponents hit an angle. Then, return that angle with the same angle. Basically, send the ball back to wherever it came from. This will often be your highest percentage shot and steadiest game. Also, you can throw your opponents off-balance by making them double-back (wrong-footed) as they're heading for the center of the court. The great backcourters, Borg and Connors, played this style of tennis to a "T."

2. Make sure to mix up your serves. Try to think of the serve your opponents might not be ready for. Slice to the center, slice wide. Hit big, flat serves right at them, off-speed "loopy" serves pulling them off the court. Keep in mind that there are numerous service possibilities (especially after you've mastered the different spins). Keep 'em guessing.

   (a) Slice: wide into the alley
   (b) Slice: jam them (at their bodies)
   (c) Flat: down the center line, or right at them
   (d) Topspin "kick" into the alley, or at their body, and so on.

3. Move your opponents from corner to corner, and wait for a short ball to come in on. Try approaching to the middle as well as to the sides. There's less angle for the passer to work with.

4. There are four definitive types of approach shots to come in on. One is a deep drive to a corner. Another is a chip (short or deep) that stays low and makes the other player hit up. You can come in on a well-disguised drop shot as well. The last is a lofty, off-pace topspin, making your opponents look up and not giving them much to work with. Try all of these approaches before you decide against the aggressive game.

5. Use finesse if your opponents are slow, can be thrown off-balance when moving, or have weak net games. Drop-shot, lob, and angle. Make your opponents play long points, moving them around in the short court and using your touch to throw them off. Some players move very well laterally, but not up and back—and vice versa.

6. Should you find yourself playing a steady backcourt player who's also proficient with the short balls and at net, then you're probably in the 5.0 division or the equivalent. Now you really have to "win," because this player is generally not going to "beat himself."

    Many would try to hit too good of a shot against this type of player. That usually results in unforced errors. Unless you're very "on," you'll end up playing below your capabilities, beating yourself. You've got to be more patient and more clever to beat the "all-court" player.

    Don't leave any of your game "in the bag." If it's a weapon of yours, then serve-and-volley, drop shot; whatever you've got, you pretty much want to use it, at least until it no longer proves to be effective.

    Finally, try playing down the middle, and go to the sides gradually, using small angles. Then widen the angle when you get the chance, and approach the net to the other side (or wrong-foot them to the same side). Try to take the net while putting your opponent on the run while he or she is off-balance.

◆   ◆   ◆

The following is a list of strategies that are conventional and not-so-conventional. It's good to look at them all and see if you can apply them to your game to broaden your philosophy about match play:

◆   Be a "chameleon." Change your game to match up against theirs.

- Learn from all player types: Use their tactics against other players.
- Approach down the line.
- Volley cross-court.
- Hit where they ain't.
- Play down the middle. Return an angle with an angle.
- Overhead down the line, unless they're standing or running there.
- Moonball, or drop-shot as an approach shot— the element of surprise.
- Vary your serve the way a pitcher would vary his pitches.
- Save your best serve for big points.
- If you can, take away their best shot, then hit to their weakness to "close out" the point.
- Topspin-serve, cross-court volley (or volley back behind them: wrong-footed).
- Look to wrong-foot your opponent, as well as hit away from them.
- Return a drop shot with a drop shot.
- When in doubt, serve to the body.
- In general, return serves down the middle, unless their serve is a "sitter."
- Don't forget to find out if your opponent can hit all the shots. Keep looking. You'll always uncover a weak spot. Expose and exploit as many weaknesses as possible.
- Know if your opponent's a lefty, righty, or ambidextrous. It happens.
- Defensive-lob when you're in trouble. It gives you extra time (to get back into the point).
- Don't relax (or play it too safe) when you're up in the match. That's when your opponent may turn it on.
- Never change a winning game.
- Always change a losing game.
- Get to net, especially if it's worked for you against that player previously.
- Better to hit deep than hard.

♦ Get your first serve in!
♦ Don't go for the lines.

General Points to Remember During Match Play

♦ Don't be impressed with your opponent's great shots until after the match. This will surely diminish your confidence, and give you a less-than-100 percent mentality, adding pressure.

♦ On big points and big games, don't overhit serves or returns. Open the point with a solid serve or return. Keep the ball coming back, down the middle. No gifts, please.

♦ Those crucial pre-game minutes: Note your opponent's game (and your strengths), and come up with a "game plan." You can refer back to this plan during the course of the match. Develop a "warm-up" that gets you (mentally and physically) prepared.

♦ Run before you practice. Remember to side-step (both sides), back-pedal, and sprint. You might want to get ready to work out by running the lines of the court. Get ready to move. Also, do some high-stepping and some butt-kicking.

♦ Take time between changeovers; doing so can help *you* while distracting *them.*

♦ Bring what you need nutritionally to a match, such as bananas and fresh water.

♦ Learn how to "breathe to win." Remember: if you stop breathing, you die! Start the day with your stretching and breathing. Grunting at the hit works for many players and gets them to exhale.

◆ As Jimmy Connors once said, "Pressure represents opportunity. The greater the pressure, the greater the opportunity. And I love opportunity!" Enjoy and welcome each challenge with enthusiasm, anticipation, and faith.

◆ Unless you know that your opponent's serve is an awesome weapon, always elect to receive first. It starts your opponent off with pressure and makes him wonder, "Why does he want me to serve first? Does he think he's going to start with a break?" The principle here is that it gets your opponent to ponder and possibly raises doubts.

◆ Never be surprised! Expect your opponent to play his or her very best. Don't ever assume a ball is not coming back.

◆ When you've got players on the ropes, expect them to come out like snarling cats who are backed into a corner. They'll come out fighting, scratching, and clawing. At match game and match point, your opponents will come out faster and tougher, making fewer mistakes and more great shots. They're not going to lay down and die, so don't go to sleep.

◆ Again: Be aggressive at critical points and games, especially at "closing time." Don't play it too safe, because they'll come back. I see it time and time again. Go for your shots, yet don't overhit. Serve-and-volley. Chip-and-charge, or hit a solid return. Three-quarter speed is the rule. Play your game.

◆ Move your feet and breathe. Make yourself dangerous. Stay involved with the game!

Never Underestimate the Power of Momentum

Here's a story that illustrates the awesome power of momentum:

> Billy, my doubles partner, and I were down 7-6, 5-7, love-3, to the number-one (undefeated) doubles team from Redlands, California. It was the last match of the day, so it was kind of the highlighted grudge match. Billy was serving at love-30, and even though we were playing all right, we weren't converting the big points. It wasn't looking good for us in the third, when, miraculously, everything changed.
>
> Billy hit his first volley close to the sideline, and the ball was called out. Well, Billy didn't like that call, and he let them know it. "Bull___!" he yelled. The guy who made the call had played Billy just an hour before in a heated singles match, which Billy had lost 7-5 in the third, and this guy boldly retorted, "Hey, Billy, I've had enough of your sh__!"
>
> The next thing I know, my partner is taking his aluminum racket over his head as if he's going to haul it at the guy. I'm in total disbelief. I probably just sat there with my mouth agape, I don't remember. Billy faked the throw (thank God), and this guy jumps over the net and goes after my partner. I don't know exactly how it happened, but both teams, coaches, and students unloaded onto our court, in an absolute melee. Unbelievable! There must have been two dozen people out on the court. It was like a hockey game!
>
> Finally, after about eight minutes, the crowd got back to their seats, and we got back to the match. Nobody was physically injured. But now we couldn't miss, and they couldn't hit. It was amazing—we won the first eight points, hitting about as well as we could. We felt good. We had renewed energy and new life. Our otherwise worthy opponent seemed a step shy and just a little "off." We went on to win the match 6-4 in the third.

◆   ◆   ◆

I didn't tell you this story to advocate the use of profanity and violence, but merely to show that no one knows why the momentum shifts suddenly, and why certain matches ebb and flow. Momentum is an elusive concept, but don't underestimate its presence and its power. Anything can happen.

In short, trust and stay with your momentum. Don't all of a sudden play it safe. Really hit your shots. Dictate the pace. Move at your desired speed, which will generally be brisk.

On the other hand, if you need to gain momentum, keep the ball coming back over the net, and start making your shots. You can always turn a match around. Play within yourself. Don't let your opponent dictate the pace. Tie your shoe. Anything! Just do something to slow down the pace. Your opponents want to get off the court as quickly as possible. Don't let them.

Control the match energy. Before every serve give your opponent a look that says, "I'm going to win this point."

◆　◆　◆　◆　◆

Chapter Twelve

CONDITION YOUR MIND, BODY, AND SOUL

Condition to Win!

Knowing that you're in better physical condition than your opponent can give you tremendous confidence, especially in long matches and big tournaments. Confidence is a strong and empowering mindset. There is no question that you play best when you play from strength, and that inner power comes about when you're in a confident state of mind.

In the quarterfinals of the boys 18-and-unders in the New England Championships, I played against a big hitter named Paul when I was 17. He was ranked in the top five, and I was ranked about #11 in New England. He hit harder (and better) than I did and had much more confidence in his game. Nonetheless, I wanted the win badly, so I studied his game the day before, when he easily won in straight sets. He didn't watch my match, because frankly, he wasn't too worried about me.

I took him to three sets by working the game plan I had formulated, which was to get him frustrated by returning his big shots. I was playing well, and I realized that if I kept it up, I could win! I was making him hit at least three potential winners a point. I ran everything down, sometimes returning three and four overheads in a point. (We were playing on red clay, a very slow surface, which was to my advantage.) However, as hard as I was working, I got down love-3 in the third. Then at the court changeover, it hit me.

The night before at the big tournament party, I had seen this guy drinking some beer and smoking a couple of cigarettes. I had left the party and gone to bed early that night because I was pumped up to pull off the upset. The next day, I got up early so I could stretch, run, and get psyched for the match.

Down 5-7, 7-5, love-3 in the third, I noticed definite signs of fatigue in Paul when we were changing sides. I started thinking about his smoking and drinking the night before, and I also thought about how I had been training all summer, and that this was the biggest tournament in New England! I knew I was more ready on this particular day than he was, and my conditioning would not let me down. At that moment I thought that if I could keep him out on the court in the hot summer sun (90 degrees and East Coast "muggy"), I could wear him down and still win this match.

Well, that's exactly what I did. I played harder as the match wore on—running for more balls, and making more great gets than I had in the first two sets (maybe in my life!). The match lasted over three-and-a-half hours. I came back and won 7-5 in the third, after being down two match points. My conditioning and my faith pulled me through. Those two things always pay off.

Stay Physically Fit

Staying in shape enables you to execute all of the components of your game consistently. Conditioning gets you to the ball more quickly and more often. It also helps you finish the stroke on-balance. Sometimes, a match comes down to who's in better physical condition. Your tennis will be directly affected by your foot speed, strength, endurance, and ability to react.

So, stay in shape. It gives you confidence. There are so many excellent training programs that it would be impossible to do them justice in one book. However, I'll give you a few training ideas that you can work off of. I suggest you find a program that works for you and stick to it, and/or upgrade as necessary. Your program should encompass the four physical areas of conditioning: aerobic (cardiovascular), strength, endurance, and flexibility.

Michael Chang purportedly runs through a water-filled swimming pool to increase speed, strength, and endurance. At the University of North Carolina, we used to run the stadium steps over and over. I used to see Chris Evert play on hot Florida days wearing a full set of sweats. I've seen Ramash Krishnan (a former world-ranked pro) do over 400 "double-jumps" (bringing a jump rope around twice for each jump) in a row! (I only got up to about 100.)

Just remember that your program must be a slow, steady build-up in all areas if you want to avoid injuries. Stretching must be made a part of any workout if you're serious about your health. *Take the time to stretch!*

The following are just a couple of suggestions for you to review and possibly add to your tennis program. They are the minimum requirements for staying in shape if you're really serious about your physical development.

The Recreational Player:

◆ Jog or walk three times per week.
◆ Stretch five to ten minutes every morning and again before bed.

The Tournament Player:

◆ Run three days per week (one to three miles).
◆ Run three days per week, for speed. Do line drills, "butterflies" (running along the lines of the court), sprints, and jump rope.
◆ Stretch (yoga) daily 10 to 20 minutes (more during the tournament season).

- ◆ Weight-train three to four times per week during the "off" season. Back off weights during tournaments, as it could negatively affect your "touch."
- ◆ Do push-ups and sit-ups at least three to four days per week

The Open Player:

- ◆ Run six to seven days per week for speed and endurance.
- ◆ Stretch twice a day 20 to 40 minutes at a time.
- ◆ Engage in a rigorous weight-training program four days per week during the off-season.
- ◆ Constantly do push-ups and sit-ups. Run wherever you go.

Swimming is an excellent all-around exercise for strength, endurance, and flexibility, but I've found that it can make your muscles feel "extra-long," and throw off your "touch" and racket control. Swim during the off-season, just to be safe.

Staying in shape should be a full-time job and a way of life. My college doubles partner and I used to run everywhere—to classes, parties—everywhere on campus. When we were hanging out watching TV or talking on the phone, we would stretch (and I still do). Staying in shape is a habit.

Tennis Is an Aerobic Sport

The greater the demands, the greater the preparation needed. Lateral movement and your first step to the ball are the two things you want to constantly work on. So, when you run or jog, make sure you include side-stepping, back-pedaling, crossover stepping, and sprinting in your workout.

Tennis is a game of quick starts and stops. Recovery time, agility, and strength are vital. So often matches come down to one or two great gets. Look at how Michael Chang wins. Almost every time people speak about him, the first things they mention are his speed and awesome physical stamina. You can make up for many shortcomings with strength, speed, and endurance, coupled with faith and desire.

Cardiovascular conditioning can also be done off-court. Cross-training, yoga, surfing, basketball, and soccer are great for physical conditioning with respect to balance, footwork, timing, and endurance. Agassi has recommended cross-training in other sports in order to improve your tennis game. I agree.

Engage in a Strengthening and Stretching Program

Most players should be developing some kind of strengthening program, be it weightlifting or isometrics. Always remember, it's the quality and intensity of the training that counts—not just the duration. Exercise in the same manner that you play tennis: with passion. And when building strength, be careful. Weightlifting can be dangerous, so build slowly! Find a trainer—someone who knows what he or she is doing, to help you.

Along with strengthening, serious stretching can also help reduce injuries. Knees, wrists, shoulders, rotator cuffs, ankles, forearms, stomach, and back should all be strengthened and stretched. Strengthen the muscles around the joints! You see a lot of "jocks" out there just working on bigger shoulders and chests. Playing tennis requires more than looking good. Stretching is a crucial element of a total fitness program. It makes you quicker, stronger, and an all-around better athlete. I've found Ashtanga yoga to be the best and most complete conditioning program. It strengthens your mind as well as your body. And when done properly, it can be quite aerobic. It is deep, aggressive stretching with an emphasis on vigorous breathing (called *pranayama*). Yoga can help you become more focused and aware of your body; and as illustrated in Chapter Two, it can improve your overall focus.

Play Tennis!

Playing tennis requires a great deal of muscle memory. Remember, practice does not make perfect. *Perfect* practice makes perfect. Good-quality repetition is important when developing your game and building the appropriate "muscle memory." There are always people you can drill with, and a few tennis clubs have good workout programs for serious players. Find them.

Practice like you want to play a match. Be enthusiastic. Move your feet. Run, don't walk, to pick up the balls. Ilie Nastase (number one in the early seventies) used to say that the best way to get in tennis shape is to *play tennis*. There's a lot of truth in that statement. Play tennis to get in tennis shape; play matches and drill. Tennis is a unique sport, so even if you feel you're in good running or "lifting" shape, remember that tennis is different. Your movements and physical requirements are not quite like any other sport. You might be able to walk ten miles or play five games of basketball, but that doesn't necessarily mean you can go three hard sets.

Eat to Win

A truly efficient tennis player must pay attention to diet. A high-carbohydrate diet the day before a match will give a player energy throughout. A sensible diet without simple sugars (candy and "junk" food, yet high in carbohydrates), is probably ideal for most. But everyone's needs are different. The point to remember is that you're pushing yourself to perform at your highest level, so fill your engine with appropriate amounts of the best fuel. Know what's right for you, and maintain your will power.

I like to put "high-octane" fuel in my body: natural foods that are rich in nutrients. No refined sugars, no grease, and no long scientific words such as "monosodium glutamate."

Stay Mentally Sharp

Mental conditioning separates the erratic players from those in the "winning habit." Focus is the eventual result of mental conditioning. You have to be able to concentrate on the ball and the game throughout the match—match after match. This means learning to clear your mind of the daily clutter, and to focus on the present—whether you're stretching at home, drilling on the court, staring at a tennis ball, or whatever.

Concentration isn't something you can turn on and off like a faucet. It's a skill. It's something you have to develop. Concentration is also a key element in other parts of life. Make a habit out of meditating and positive visualization. Practice the art of relaxation. Learn to think on and off the court.

Practice like you play. Why practice differently than you'd play in a match? Get in the habit of being hungry and staying focused on every point and on each ball. Try to get and stay in the winning habit. Play with passion. When Andre Agassi was asked, in a *60 Minutes* interview, what "cuts it when you're at 30-all in the fifth set in front of 18,000 people who are not necessarily pulling for you," he replied: "Your desire to want to be nowhere else."

That attitude and desire should be with you in all of your life's endeavors. Create and maintain a positive environment for your "self." Treat your mind, body, and soul with deep respect. Don't overeat, over-drink, or overreact. Life is good!

Feed Your Soul

When engaging in competition, don't wait a few games to get "into the match," and don't drift once you're there. Do your best. Use all your tools.

Meditation is a key component of mental conditioning. Getting over pre-match jitters or butterflies requires slowing down your breathing and relaxing. This is the precise principle that meditation is based on. You concentrate your mental energy on the match ahead as you breathe deeply and calm yourself.

You can also use this meditation time to get your confidence up. Say to yourself: "I'm a winner; I believe in myself." Some people need this time to not only relax and get focused, but to actually get pumped up. If you're the type who tends to get nervous and "psyched out," use your meditation time to play out the match in your head. Visualize yourself playing and winning points. "See" exactly how you'd like the match to turn out. As I've said before, proper visualization can serve as a dress rehearsal that's as effective as an actual practice session. Meditation also helps you focus by training your mind to think deeply on one topic.

You have to find the right combination of mental calmness and competitive aggression. Julie, one of my students, a scrappy player who enjoys playing the baseline and running balls down, believes she can actually be too calm for a match. Her high-energy style requires her to get "pumped up" so she can be extremely aggressive and use her speed whenever possible.

Her pre-match routine involves getting centered through meditation and getting herself fired up for the task ahead. Through trial and error, she's learned what makes her focus and play her best, and then she puts it to work on a habitual basis. This routine helps her continually grow as a player, with few setbacks.

Look Like a Winner!

Playing tennis isn't work. It's play. Work is going to your job. Even tough drilling should be something you look forward to. Enjoy your time on the court. Embrace it. Relish the process of learning, growing, dedicating and improving yourself. Knowing what you're doing out there will build your confidence; and confidence is the name of the game when you're playing to win. Let your attitude shine through.

Get into the habit of believing in yourself and your game. As a positive, energetic, centered individual, *you* make things happen—things don't just happen *to* you. Bad luck or a bad draw shouldn't ruin your experience. Just play the ball, and do your best. A balanced person learns from every experience and doesn't get rattled by one poor performance. Maintain a light-hearted approach to the game, and you'll never feel let down. Remember: No excuses...no emotions (except for positive ones)...and no ego!

You can even do a form of quick meditation while you're preparing to serve. Think about a time when you were your happiest and most at ease. It can actually help you relax, at least long enough to hit your serve. You'll find that this can be a powerful source for drawing out a positive feeling and, thus, your best efforts. Deepak Chopra, the renowned medical doctor/metaphysician, says that people will salivate just by *thinking* about eating a lemon. So, use your mind to help you visualize that win!

Look like a winner (not a whiner) always! Keep your head up. Maintain a pleasant expression. Never look down at your feet. Don't be afraid to speak up if the ball is out, but don't be rude or abusive. Never drag your racket on the ground or moan after you've missed an easy shot. Keep your spirits high and light. Respect your racket, your opponent, and your self. Endurance, concentration, and simply enjoying the total experience will make every tennis match, practice session, and drill a pleasurable experience.

Have fun!

Chapter Thirteen

LEARN AND GROW

The world of tennis is a place to learn and grow as an athlete and as a human being throughout your life. Once you've crossed over into that realm where you're thinking and acting like a "player," you begin to play like one. Tennis becomes a form of meditation (in motion) and a reflection of your inner self. Terms like focus, discipline, and humility take on more profound and personal meanings. Use your tennis to enhance your life, on and off the court.

Once you've "crossed over," I suggest that you keep a pen and paper in your tennis bag. There's a lot that goes on, on the court; and there's even more that goes on in your head. Be open to it all, but stay focused on your new fundamentals. Jot things down that you notice about yourself when you're playing well.

Every time you play tennis, you build on the time before—it's a cumulative effect. Every time you stretch, you strengthen and improve your overall body and your focus. You are responsible for your own game, so acquire good tennis habits. This game is not just an outlet for releasing your physical tensions and for competing against others—it's a form of mental and spiritual awareness. It's special.

◆　◆　◆

Tennis Heroes/Tennis Casualties

What follows are a few stories that I've lived myself, or that I've witnessed, which help to explain the power and importance of the game. I think that there are lessons to be learned here, so take whatever you need and apply it to your own life.

◆ ◆ ◆

True "all-court" players have satisfied and mastered the physical, mental, and emotional components of the game. They are the tennis heroes. On the other hand, there are those whose fortunes have risen and fallen and whose stories make one cringe. They are the tennis casualties.

The Rise and Fall of a Junior Star

When Becky first came to me as a student, she had never won a round in a sanctioned tournament. She hadn't even fared well in the local satellite junior events. She was 14 and loved to play the game. In fact, playing tennis was the only thing Becky wanted to do. She wanted to be a pro.

A very gifted athlete, and quite intelligent, Becky was simply lacking in sound fundamentals, which were easy enough for her to attain in about four months. She went on to win her first Southern California-sanctioned tournament about six months after she started with me. Things continued to go well for another three tournaments—she won all of them. But that was the beginning of the end.

I noticed that her father was starting to put an enormous amount of pressure on both Becky and me to continue her winning ways. She began to get more and more agitated on and off the court, especially when she was competing. She didn't have the same enthusiasm to play tournaments or to practice. Her father seemed to get more involved and active, though, at the same rate that his daughter was reaching her "burn-out" point. I tried to explain to him that he had to back off and give Becky room "to grow." Tennis is a sport you play alone, with only your feelings and insecurities. Becky had to play for herself and for her pure love of the game.

My advice to Becky's father wasn't heeded, though, and Becky eventually reached the breaking point. Her father had driven her to a big tournament in L.A., where she was, for the third time, the number-one seed. Becky's father looked at the competition, brushed them off, and told his daughter that she didn't have to play a tough match "until the finals." When I heard that, I was livid. I told her father (out of Becky's earshot) that he had just given her the kiss of death and that there was no way she'd win the tournament that day. The way he glared at me, I knew my days as Becky's coach were numbered.

Becky struggled to win her first match of the day 6-3, 7-6. She lost later that afternoon, in the second round, to a girl who was decent, but unseeded, and certainly not the player Becky was. It was ugly: 3-6, 6-2, 0-6. She "lost it" all right—she was warned twice for poor sportsmanship, and she came off the court crying.

Making matters worse, in our next—and last—lesson, I asked Becky about her attitude, why she was getting so upset out there. What she told me made me want to cry. She said, "You know, I liked it better when I sucked." I asked her what she meant, and she explained, "Everyone thinks I'm supposed to win all the time. I don't think I'm that good." Basically, Becky was the first case of "fear of success" I had ever personally encountered—but certainly not the last.

Becky never wanted to practice or play matches after that—not with the passion she once had. She disappeared from the tournament scene about as quickly as she arrived on it. Every once in a while, I'd see her name on a tournament draw, but she never won another tournament. She gained a reputation for being a tank (someone who doesn't even try to win), who happened to have great strokes.

Here is someone who really loved the game, but who got side-tracked by expectations and outside pressures. What a shame. Take heed, parents.

◆ ◆ ◆

"...words like expectation *and* potential *and* pressure *and* doubts. *You know, it seems like they're all over the place, like land mines you can just step on, and out of nowhere can just blow up. And everything can come crashing down, ya know—in the middle of a match, in the middle of putting your heart on the line. And that's scary. It's scary because you come off the court and you feel like a failure."*

— Andre Agassi, during a "60 Minutes" interview in 1995

◆ ◆ ◆

Always a Champion

My doubles partner, Billy, and I were making one of our many comebacks, playing at a local tournament in Long Beach, California. We played against a good college player and some 15- or 16-year-old kid with a steady game and a two-handed backhand. We, of course, played the kid hard, and he wasn't half-bad.

In fact, this kid ran everything down and didn't miss much, and he had a decent serve. No big deal. He knew we were "playing" him, but he didn't get offended or intimidated, even when we hit shots right at him, hard. He was a real gentleman about it all. He kept quiet and played ball.

The duo beat us something like 6-4, 6-4, in a good, high-energy match. We both commented on the ride home what a "together" kid that teenager was, and how he remained solid and unrattled throughout the match. We both mentioned that we felt no shame or anger about losing to a kid who played like that. Two years later, Billy called me up and excitedly told me to watch that kid in the finals of the U.S. Open. Pete Sampras was a gentleman and a champion, then and now. Hey, when you've got it, you've really got it!

◆　◆　◆

Sometimes, the Man Eats the Bear...

Quarterfinals of the NCAA Championships, Division 3. Billy and I were playing the best match of our lives. We had spent the last two days battling, down match points, but we came back, and we decided it was destiny.

We were up 6-4, 4-2, playing virtually flawless tennis against the number-one seeds. But it seemed as if the match turned around in a split-second, and we were down 5-4 in the third after losing the second 7-6. We got it together and tied it at 5-all and then 6-6. We went up 4-1 in the tie-break. Those guys played incredible, unbelievable tennis. This is supposed to be Division Three! Big crowd, big tennis. They went up 6-5.

Serving, I got my first one in, hard to the backhand corner, ad side, and came in behind it. My opponent mishit the return badly, and Billy let the ball fly out. But it stayed in! I dropped to my knees, weak with disappointment.

Sometimes you have to take the bad with the good, and you somehow have to learn to love it all, at least when you look back.

...And Sometimes the Bear Eats the Man

◆　◆　◆

A Psychological Game

My student Erica, a Southern California top 10-ranked woman, recently told me an interesting story about a match that she had barely won. She was trying out one of the new, long-body rackets.

She played a first round with it and lost the first set, and then she switched back to her own trusty "stick" (racket). She came back and won the second set, playing a little better. She went back out on the court and won the first game of the third. She was up 30-love when she noticed that she was playing with the longer racket, the wrong one! She had obviously picked it up inadvertently at the changeover.

That was it! She couldn't play a lick after that. She lost the next two games with that racket and went on to lose the third 6-2. Of course, at that point in the match Erica was confused and upset, seeing that time was running out and she didn't know which racket she played best with.

Moral of the story: It's not the stick that makes the woman. If she had been truly focused, she could have played with a broomstick!

◆　◆　◆

By the way, in the first sanctioned singles tournament I ever won, I played the finals with my brother-in-law's cheap aluminum racket because both of mine were stolen the day before. Play the ball, not the racket.

Respect Your Opponent:
It Will Improve Your Win/Loss Record

Never take anyone too lightly. Have respect for your opponents. They're out there trying their best, putting it on the line, too. Respect them because they're giving you another opportunity to compete.

Other than for the obvious moral reasons, there are also practical ones to maintain respect for others. There are several juniors whom I've met who stumbled upon this rule of respect the hard way. They improved, got a ranking, and unfortunately they "read their own press." That's when the inevitable happened.

They played opponents who they thought were no good, or not as good as they are, and they gave them no respect. Maybe they even told their friends that the match should be "easy" or "over with" in a hurry. Or maybe, they just looked ahead to the later rounds.

What almost always happened then, is that the opponents made some great gets, played well overall, and "caught them cold." They took the lead because their cocky opponents had no respect for them. And the offshoot of that was: these players lost respect for themselves. They lost confidence and energy, and those losing feelings could be instantly picked up on by their opponents.

Energy and momentum transfer that easily and quickly. The tables are turned, and suddenly the sure winners are the certain losers.

So, respect your opponents. Then you can...

...Respect Your "Self"

Don't let anyone take advantage of you or intimidate you. Do your thing before the match, play your game during the match, and respect yourself as a competitor, a tennis player, and a human being.

Make the right call as soon as you see it. Don't get talked out of anything. Your opponents have the right to challenge you, but you have the right to hold your ground if you know you're right. No "trash-talking," though. Don't let anyone put you down, and don't you do it to them. Mutual respect will bring out the best in you and your tennis.

Always look like the winner no matter what the score. No tantrums, whining, or racket throwing. Have respect for your surroundings, your equipment, your self and most of all...

...Respect the Game

The fact that you got to this point in the book tells me that you love the game of tennis. That love should manifest itself through a continual and habitual respect for this magnificent game.

Respect your coaches and teachers, but learn to differentiate between reality and hype. I mean, it's not always the coach with the most students, or the one who charges the most for lessons who's necessarily the best. Does your coach take the time to explain the minute aspects of the game, or does he or she teach only from one side of the court?

Watch how your coach's players play and act. Do they have good form and nice strokes? Do they keep the ball in play in a match? Do they have good second serves, or do they double-fault? Are they cool and polite, or are they racket-throwers and babies? How's their mental and emotional stability and toughness? Do they come from behind, or do they blow leads? Do they play well under pressure? Are they in the winning habit?

Respect the game enough to give back to the game. Play with players who truly love tennis and who want to improve—for themselves, and not just for parents, friends, and peers. Play with those who are better than you are, but also practice as much as you can, so also play with those who are trying to rise to your level. Help others improve. Make the game a better sport for everyone involved in it.

Love the competition. Don't ever "duck it." As Jimmy Conners said time and time again: The bigger (and more pressure) the point (the challenge), the greater the opportunity; and Jimmy loved opportunity. Love the opportunities, and take the challenges. Get all you can out of the game.

Faith, Not Fear

Finally, play out of faith, not fear. Go for the win, and don't worry about losing. Play a game that you enjoy, one you feel proud of. Compete to the last point and with your last drop of energy. It ain't over till the last point is played. (This I've encountered through countless personal experiences.)

Remember, the net and the lines are not your enemies or boundaries. They're your friends, your guides, helping to steer you to a better game.

Take your tennis with you into all aspects of your life. It's not just a game. It's a sport and an arena where your wit, self-reliance, strength, determination, and courage are all tested each time you step on the court. Build these areas of yourself through your tennis. You'll find that rhythm, balance, timing, as well as other tennis fundamentals, apply to life as a whole. Stay relaxed, healthy, and focused in order to enhance your every day and every moment on this Earth! *You are the ultimate winner!*

Congratulations!

AFTERWORD

When I was 26 years old, I applied for my first non-tennis job, with AT&T Information Systems. I was competing with over 300 applicants for two positions. The job was selling mainframe computers and phone systems, about which I knew absolutely nothing.

To my amazement, I got the job, and several weeks after I started, I asked Charlie, my boss, why he gave me the position. He told me that it was because I played college tennis. I'm sure I gave him a quizzical look, because he continued that he had wanted to play on his college tennis team but wasn't good enough.

He told me that he had always admired good tennis players because they had mastered such an all-encompassing sport. He said that he knew that anyone who could play that kind of tennis must be a dedicated and disciplined individual, with a passion for winning and for life.

I did a good job in my "suit." But of course, I had to return to tennis, my first love.

MY STORY:
JWB's JOURNEY TO TENNIS
ENLIGHTENMENT

The information I've presented in this book is about today's tennis, which is much different than when I was playing junior tournaments with a Jack Kramer wood racket. Tennis was all about style—whether you played "straight back" or the "big loop," and so forth. It emphasized consistency, placement, and touch, especially with the tennis elite, who included Bjorn Borg, Jimmy Connors, and Guillermo Vilas—all very interesting and cunning backcourt players.

Today's game is more about contact and focus. Hitting forehands off either foot, open or closed, is not only practical, but it is mandatory in the higher ranks of the game. The game is all about light rackets that can generate most of the power if used correctly and efficiently. Today, anyone who enjoys the game can play. Yet, on the other hand, people seem to get complacent when they reach a certain level, rather than pushing themselves to play up to their highest potential.

I have been fortunate to have coached many players, some from the first time they picked up a racket, through the college and professional ranks. I coached 10-year-old "junior pros" to men's 55-and-over champions. Through my coaching and my own personal experiences with tournament tennis, I've discovered what brings out the best in all levels and ages of players. With all due modesty, I have to say that I know how to make any man or woman *look and feel more like a real player.*

◆　◆　◆

My tennis background began in the late sixties in Connecticut, where tennis was a seasonal sport—only being played three months a year. Starting at age 11, I was a relatively late starter. The first three years I only played in the summers (when it wasn't raining, that is). The other nine months I played soccer, basketball, baseball, and ice hockey;

I also played touch football, wrestled, and sledded (in the snow). Basically I played just about anything—even sports that my friends and I invented. It didn't matter what sport it was—I always loved to play.

The juniors provided me with some basic techniques and tournament experience. I was a serious student and worked very hard, being that I had a lot of catching up to do. My coach, Jon Nogrady, was a technical fanatic who taught looping flat groundstrokes and a very Eastern, conservative game. He taught many of the ranked players in the area, among them a world-class player, Paul Gerken. During my early years, my coaches (Nogrady and Peter Chang), believed in me, and I had a strong belief in myself, but I certainly was not a *player.*

I achieved New England rankings during my last three years of the juniors (at ages 16, 17, and 18) in both singles and doubles. My best rankings were in the top ten. I only won a handful of sanctioned singles tournaments, with just a few big wins that I usually "scrapped" out. I still wasn't a player who could dominate a match; nor was I an "all-court" player. I had a bad temper and had a great deal of trouble staying relaxed and focused throughout a match.

It seemed like there were two types of tennis players in those days—either serious players from tennis families, or "club hackers," kids that just fooled around at the game. I was serious about the game, without having experience, so I was caught in uncharted waters. Somehow, I was always in a situation where I was in over my head. Other people, even "players," always thought that I was better than I was, because I "looked" like a player, had a few good wins, and always made great gets. Deep down, though, I knew I wasn't one of them. I knew I was just a very good "club" player.

At age 17, I represented New England at the Junior Nationals in Kalamazoo, Michigan, and in other national tournaments. Although I was relatively inexperienced and I knew that I didn't really belong there, it was still a dream come true. I got to see and play with the best players in the world—when they were kids. Vitas Gerulaitis, Jimmy Connors, Gene Mayer—they all played there. It's a time I'll never forget. That was the kind of tennis I wanted to play.

Then it was down to Harry Hopman's International Tennis Academy in Florida. This was the biggest and best school in the world.

And unlike Nick Bollettieri, Hopman knew first-hand what it took to play and win. He had been a player, coached the Australian Davis Cup for Years, and was respected by all the greats: Fred Stolle, John Newcombe, Rod Laver, Ken Rosewall, and so on.

This place was so impressive. It was huge—tennis courts and players everywhere! I was excited to finally become a player! I thought, cocky kid that I was, that I had experience at the national level, so two weeks of solid training was all I needed! I wish!

I must admit that I did get in the best shape of my life—I really learned about hard work and tennis drills! However, by the end of two weeks, I hadn't improved my game one bit—perhaps my timing was better, but that was about it. I could hit balls on the run, but I forgot how to hit the ones that came right to me, especially those with no pace. In fact, after I returned to Connecticut, I had one of the worst losses of my life! I was so depressed about my game that I just walked around in a daze for hours, wondering, Why? Why? How is this possible?! I was supposed to be better now. I was supposed to be a real player!

Training camps, in general, can only help the "real players" unless the instruction is top-notch—and that depends on each individual coach. It's unfortunate, though, because when players work so hard and then don't improve, they get discouraged and sometimes quit the game! I didn't like that then, and I don't like it now. Discouraging players is the greatest crime that any coach or institution can commit in the game of tennis!

Never aspiring to world-class status in the juniors, my quest for "my game" continued—in college. My first two years of school were spent playing #8 varsity singles, at best, for the University of North Carolina at Chapel Hill. I was once again in over my head, for my limited experience and talent. Don Skakle, my coach at the time, knew it.

During the off-season, we did physical conditioning, lifted weights, played basketball, and ran around the track in full sweats. It was great to be on the team and to be treated like a nationally acclaimed collegiate player! I got to eat at the "training table," which always had the best food in town, and I got to live in one of the only coed dorms (another big plus) on campus—"the jock dorm."

The season consisted of about an hour-and-a-half of sprinting, jogging, isometrics, push-ups, leg-lifts, and sit-ups. We would then play tennis for two-and-a-half hours. This was our daily routine unless we had a match. There was virtually no technical training or instruction. *(By the time you get to college, you better be a player or forget it!)* So, basically, what I learned in my first two years of college was a lot about getting in physical shape, as I had previously done at Hopman's. I still didn't know the game, and this approach wasn't helping any. Once again, this whole routine was geared to *players!*

I decided to take a semester off school and see if I could find my game on the pro circuit, since I still had the faith and desire. My parents (reluctantly) supported my decision, and I was off to Florida to play a satellite circuit called the Watch Tour. The experience I gained was invaluable. My new Florida coach and mentor, Gery Groslimond, was the first real "player" I had taken lessons from, and he knew more about tournament tennis than anyone I had encountered up to that point. He was an "all-court" player who played top four on the varsity at Stanford. He was the type of player I wanted to be.

Gery was a footwork fanatic. He changed me to a semi-Western grip, shortened my stroke a bit, and taught me the importance of footwork. We did footwork drills every day for about four months, and I *did* get better. It seemed that the more I focused on footwork, the better my strokes got. I found that interesting. I must admit that footwork was probably the first thing that I really understood about the game.

During this semester off of school, I also began taking Transcendental Meditation (TM), and started to broaden my view of tennis and life. I started to understand a little about the psychological side of the game. That's when I read my first metaphysical book called *Psycho-Cybernetics,* by Maxwell Maltz, M.D. (a book Gery said was required reading for the Stanford tennis team). I found that meditating actually seemed to help my tennis, or at least my demeanor, both on and off the court. I also enjoyed learning to relax off the court and escape from tennis and other things that were on my mind, because at this point, tennis was becoming an obsession, no longer just a game. I mean, look where I was: out of school, on the pro tour, living somewhere in Florida, losing in the early rounds.

I did play some of the best tennis of my life, but I still wasn't steady enough or hitting with enough pace to do any damage on the tour. It was a war out there. This was not the juniors, I realized. Nor was it college ball. This was the big time! These guys were playing for their wives and kids. I won a few, and lost more. I was always on the lookout for anything that seemed to make tennis sense to me. I still didn't know how to master the game without an extraordinary amount of practice. I felt doomed, as if the only way to play this game was to be "pushed," starting at a very young age, which of course was no longer possible for me.

So, from that time onward I set my sights on coaching myself. Anything that made sense, I would jot down (in a journal) and try out. I realize now that I was developing this book way back then. My doubles partner, Weldon Rogers, a high-ranking black player in the American Tennis Association (which was an almost entirely black tennis organization since the U.S.P.T.A. wouldn't let in blacks at that time), and other practice partners had a wealth of information that they were generous in sharing with me. "You learn more from your losses," they told me. That statement alone should have made me the smartest player in the world! Anyway, I started to become a coaching fanatic, trying to put together a comprehensive tennis program for myself.

I decided that I'd better get back to college or I'd end up being a bum on the street talking about how I "coulda been a contendah" on the professional tennis tour. I transferred to the University of California at San Diego.

I worked the next two summers for the World Championship of Tennis (W.C.T.) club in Atlanta, Georgia, teaching and occasionally running their tennis camps. Here we utilized the teaching methods we learned from Dennis Van der Meer's school. I was impressed. The instruction even made sense, at least for most people, and there are still many principles that were taught there that apply to today's tennis. Certainly, for that time, it was the most sound teaching method that I had encountered. It was missing the tennis nuances and specialties that I had come to learn out on the tour and in my other experiences, but it seemed like a good place for beginners.

So, the game was finally starting to make sense to me, and I kept writing. I had worked for the previous two summers as an assistant pro at tennis clubs in New York and Florida, but it was one summer at the W.C.T. club that I became interested in developing a teaching system that would allow anyone to become a "player," and not just the gifted athletes or the very young (and usually wealthy) kids with overly pushy tennis parents. There had to be methods for the average tennis enthusiast to use that would enable them to truly grasp the soul of the game at any age. I was 22 when I began piecing together my own game, and my own philosophy.

I worked the following summer for Harry Hopman, when the number two-ranked junior player from Central America, Eric Kruseman, asked me to coach him full-time. He, Stefan Eggmeyer (top-ranked in Europe); Loren Wallis, a local Southern California junior; and Jon Paley, #4 varsity for top-ranked UCLA, were my first four full-time protegés. So before I was ever a "club pro," I played, coached, and observed tournament champions. I took note of their progress, daily programs, and what worked and what didn't. I began to video the pros to see what the common denominators in their games and strokes were, and what was just style—and not necessarily important to their game.

Right out of college I taught in Palm Springs and then moved to Los Angeles, where I coached many top-ranked adults and juniors. I moved to San Diego, California (where I presently teach), about five years ago. My teaching underwent even more breakthroughs in development, starting with the mutilation of my playing hand. Every experience (and setback) helped me discover better teaching methods.

I continue to try to find, or create, new and simple techniques that will allow *each* of my students—no matter what their age or initial level of ability—to play their very best possible tennis—incorporating mind, body, soul—and good old-fashioned perspiration!

Today, I enjoy the game of tennis immensely every time I step on the court, with the complete confidence that I'll play at my highest level. I have no bad days. As Andre Agassi has said, "The game is important to me. Despite the pressures, despite the expectations, I love what happens inside those white lines."

I believe that everyone can play tennis, and play well, and I'm going to do everything possible to make that happen. This game deserves real *players!*

Welcome to our world!

A TRIBUTE TO...

Arthur Ashe:

Arthur, first and foremost, was a role model for the people in the inner cities and the game of tennis, giving his time and energy to the children. He was a world-class *champion*, in every sense of the word. He was exciting to watch, with a beautiful serve, and a lethal backhand. He is greatly missed.

Bobby Riggs:

I loved his antics and confidence, on and off the court. He made tennis fun for everyone. His good nature and love of sport was always a boost to the popularity of tennis.

Harry Hopman:

Harry was tough, with a real "work hard, play (tennis) hard" ethic. The Australian Davis Cup coach, he worked with the likes of Rod Laver, Ken Rosewall, Fred Stolle, Tony Roche, Roy Emerson, and more. As tough as he was, he seemed to always have a smile hidden somewhere.

Bill Tilden:

He was one of the first players to play the "attacking" game. His book, *The Game of Singles in Tennis,* was the first tennis book I ever read, and it had a very positive influence on my motivation and my game. Most of the strategies are still quite valid in today's tennis.

Vitas Gerulaitis:

Vitas was a really good guy, all-around. He was a gutsy player, with quick hands and superb footwork. He was also a great advocate of the game, bringing it to kids in the New York inner city. I always thought he was a big-hearted, genuine guy, who could make incredible gets!

Tim Gullikson:

Tim was a great player and a great coach. The fact that Pete Sampras had such a good personal and working relationship with him speaks for itself.

Pancho Gonzales:

Tough, tough, tough competitor. Pancho played aggressively, and he played to win. He fought for every point and every match. He was a tennis warrior.

These players all brought a great deal to the game of tennis—a game that loved them as much as they loved it. They gave 100 percent. They are deeply missed as players and motivators. Thanks for the memories, education, and excitement!

◆   ◆   ◆   ◆   ◆

JWB's Glossary of Terms

air out: This refers to completing the swing and finishing high on the backhand.

all-court: An accomplished player, both in the backcourt and up at net.

American twist: An extreme "kick" serve, produced by tossing way over your head, with a big knee bend.

butterflies: Running along the lines of the court.

chip-and-charge: An aggressive net-rushing strategy off of the opponent's serve.

closed-face: When the racket face is closed to the net, facing more toward the ground.

club player: Someone who plays strictly for enjoyment and exercise. This player does not possess, or strive to possess, all of the aspects that the game has to offer.

continental grip: The grip that's used almost exclusively for serves, volleys, and overheads, in between the Eastern forehand and backhand grips.

court sense: A "feel" for the game; where you need to be and what you need to do.

dinkum: A game to practice court feel and "touch."

Eastern grip: Conventional grip for both the forehand and backhand.

floating or "floaters": Refers to balls that are coming high over the net at a slow pace, usually hit with underspin.

full backhand grip: Eastern backhand grip

grooved: Having your stroke feel smooth, natural, and automatic.

hacker: A player who's not a player. Someone who gets (or tries to get) the ball over the net any way he or she can, regardless of form. This player usually ends up with "tennis elbow."

headweight: The idea of letting the head of the racket do the work, particularly on serves. It refers to leverage.

inside-out forehand: Hitting the inside of the ball making it curve away from the court à la Courier or Connors. The shot is basically flat with a little side-spin.

jump serve: A serve whereby your feet leave the ground, propelling your body weight into the ball.

junk: Excessive spins, usually with little pace.

on-balance: In control of your own body. Keeping your center of gravity in the center of your body.

on edge: Racket face is perpendicular to the court, parallel to the net.

on the rise: Taking the ball while it's still coming up from the bounce.

open-face: This is when the racket face is open to the net, facing more up to the sky, such as on a continental grip.

open-stance: This refers to hitting a forehand, stepping across with your right foot instead of the conventional left one, your feet almost parallel to the net.

opposite hand: The nondominant hand.

outside of the ball: Reaching around the ball so your strings can hit and curve the ball toward the court.

playing in the zone: Playing a match with your mind, body, and emotions in total harmony. Playing up to your full potential.

race the ball: Get to the spot you want to hit the ball from (that is, into position) before the ball does.

racket face: The plane that the racket strings create.

real player: Someone who knows what they're doing out on the court.

rocking: Shifting your weight from one foot to the other. This can refer to a service motion as well as waiting to hit the service return.

scissors-kick: A term used for jumping on overhead when the ball gets behind you, whereby your left foot is forward, and at contact, the right foot then goes forward.

sitter: A ball that's almost motionless (stopped), which you should go after with a vengeance. Don't let it drop!

split step: A hop or jump step used in all phases of the game when your opponent hits the ball. It is used for quick speed and agility.

the spot: The correct contact point for groundstrokes. The three inches where the racket face is coming up the back of the ball "on edge."

stinger: Usually this refers to a volley or chip that has underspin and power, moves quickly, and almost skids at the bounce.

stutter-stepping: Quick, tiny, up-and-down footsteps that are used to adjust and fine-tune your position to the ball.

Sundial Method: A method to ensure success on spin serves, making a hammering motion with different edges of the racket.

touch and finish: A technique to ensure good contact with the ball, whereby you break the stroke in half, first physically then in your mind. First "bump" the ball, then slowly come to a finish.

walking sleep: The state of mind real players get into when they're fully focused on the ball.

Western grip: A forehand grip that naturally produces excessive top-spin. An extremely "closed-face" grip.

Index

ABOUT THE AUTHOR

Jack W. Broudy (pronounced BROH-DEE) graduated from the University of California at San Diego, with a B.A. in Communications. He played on the professional tennis tour for two years, after six years of junior, and four years of intercollegiate tennis.

Jack is presently a teaching pro in the San Diego area. He coaches numerous Southern California-ranked players, several of whom will no doubt go on to be college and professional players.

◆　　◆　　◆

If you would like to order additional copies of
The Real Spin on Tennis,
or if you would like information about Jack Broudy's seminars,
clinics, or public speaking availability, please call, ICS Books at:

(619) 753-4119

or e-mail: **jwbtennis@aol.com**

◆　◆　◆　◆　◆

Grasp the Gear...
The Real Spin on Tennis
TeeShirts and Caps

Heavyweight T-shirts
Pre Shrunk
100% Cotton
Full Color Prints

One Size Fits All
Baseball Style Cap $ 14.95

Adult: S, M, L, XL,
Youth: M, L, $ 14.95

Please add $2.95 for shipping & handling

Send Check, Money Order or Credit Card
Information to: Jack Broudy Tennis,
121 Grandview St,
Leucadia, CA 92024
email: jwbtennis@aol.com

Allow 2 to 3
weeks for
delivery